Political Humor under Stalin

POLITICAL HUMOR UNDER STALIN

An Anthology of Unofficial Jokes and Anecdotes

Edited and with an Introduction by

DAVID BRANDENBERGER

Bloomington, Indiana, 2009

SLAVICA

Front cover montage from *USSR in Construction,* No. 3 (1939): 27.
Back cover photograph from *Sovietland* 11 (1938): 7

Library of Congress Cataloging-in-Publication Data

Political humor under Stalin : an anthology of unofficial jokes and anecdotes /
edited and with an introduction by David Brandenberger.
 p. cm.
 Includes bibliographical references.
 ISBN 978-0-89357-351-5
 1. Soviet Union--Politics and government--1936-1953--Humor. 2. Soviet
Union--Politics and government--1917-1936--Humor. 3. Communism--Soviet
Union--Humor. 4. Russian wit and humor--Translations into English. I.
Brandenberger, David.

 PN6210.P65 2009
 891.7'7008035847084 2--dc22
                                                          2009047191

Slavica Publishers   [Tel.] 1-812-856-4186
Indiana University   [Toll-free] 1-877-SLAVICA
1430 N. Willis Dr.   [Fax] 1-812-856-4187
Bloomington, IN 47404-2146   [Email] slavica@indiana.edu
USA   [www] http://www.slavica.com/

Contents

List of Illustrations vii

Acknowledgments ix

Terms and Acronyms vi

Introduction 1

Unofficial Jokes and Anecdotes of the Stalin Era 27

    The Revolution, Civil War and "War Communism" 29

    The New Economic Policy 35

    Stalin's Revolution from Above 51

    Collectivization 63

    Industrialization 75

    Everyday Life 87

    The Great Terror 107

    Storm Clouds Gather 121

    The Great Patriotic War 133

    The Early Postwar Years 139

Appendix: Jokes from the Harvard Project on the Soviet Social System 145

List of Illustrations

1. *Raboche-krest'ianskaia krasnaia armiia,* ed. El Lissitskii (Moscow: Izogiz, 1934), 289 4

2. *USSR in Construction* 4 (1940): 9 5

3. *Raboche-krest'ianskaia krasnaia armiia,* ed. El Lissitskii (Moscow: Izogiz, 1934), 161 6

4. *USSR in Construction* 6 (1939): 6 7

5. *Raboche-krest'ianskaia krasnaia armiia,* ed. El Lissitskii (Moscow: Izogiz, 1934), 174 8

6. *Raboche-krest'ianskaia krasnaia armiia,* ed. El Lissitskii (Moscow: Izogiz, 1934), 191 10

7. S. Ingulov, *Politbesedy,* 3rd ed. (Moscow: Partizdat, 1937), 311 30

8. B. Volin, *Politgramota,* 2nd ed. (Moscow: Partizdat, 1933), 237 33

9. S. Ingulov, *Politgramota,* 2nd ed. (Moscow: Partizdat, 1933), 385 36

10. S. Ingulov, *Politbesedy,* 2nd ed. (Moscow: Partizdat, 1935), 282 41

11. S. Ingulov, *Politbesedy,* 3rd ed. (Moscow: Partizdat, 1937), 107 49

12. S. Ingulov, *Politbesedy,* 3rd ed. (Moscow: Partizdat, 1937), 107 52

13. S. Ingulov, *Politbesedy,* 2nd ed. (Moscow: Partizdat, 1935), 269 54

14. S. Ingulov, *Politbesedy,* 3rd ed. (Moscow: Partizdat, 1937), 105 57

15. S. Ingulov, *Politbesedy,* 2nd ed. (Moscow: Partizdat, 1935) 291 58

16. E. Iaroslavskii, *Istoriia VKP(b),* 2nd ed. (Moscow: Partizdat, 1934), vol. 2, 289 60

17. B. Volin, *Politgramota,* 2nd ed. (Moscow: Partizdat, 1933), 235 64

18. S. Ingulov, *Politbesedy,* 2nd ed. (Moscow: Partizdat, 1935), 75 66

19. S. Ingulov, *Politgramota,* 3rd ed. (Moscow: Partizdat, 1934), 36 67

20. S. Ingulov, *Politgramota,* 2nd ed. (Moscow: Partizdat, 1933), 76 70

21. S. Ingulov, *Politgramota,* 3rd ed. (Moscow: Partizdat, 1934), 240 72

22. S. Ingulov, *Politgramota,* 3rd ed. (Moscow: Partizdat, 1934), 119 76

23. S. Ingulov, *Politgramota*, 2nd ed. (Moscow: Partizdat, 1933), 44 78

24. S. Ingulov, *Politgramota*, 3rd ed. (Moscow: Partizdat, 1934), 95 81

25. S. Ingulov, *Politgramota*, 3rd ed. (Moscow: Partizdat, 1934), 109 93

26. S. Ingulov, *Politbesedy*, third ed. (Moscow: Partizdat, 1937), 107 97

27. B. Volin, *Politgramota*, 3rd ed. (Moscow: Partizdat, 1934), 242 99

28. S. Ingulov, *Politgramota*, 3rd ed. (Moscow: Partizdat, 1934), 211 110

29. S. Ingulov, *Politgramota*, 3rd ed. (Moscow: Partizdat, 1934), 48........... 116

30. S. Ingulov, *Politbesedy*, 2nd ed. (Moscow: Partizdat, 1935), 206 125

31. S. Ingulov, *Politbesedy*, 3rd ed. (Moscow: Partizdat, 1937), 151 127

32. S. Ingulov, *Politgramota*, 3rd ed. (Moscow: Partizdat, 1934), 42 130

33. S. Ingulov, *Politbesedy*, 3rd ed. (Moscow: Partizdat, 1937), 87 132

34. S. Ingulov, *Politgramota*, 3rd ed. (Moscow: Partizdat, 1934), 69 148

35. G. Bibikov, *Minin i Pozharskii* (Moscow: Gos. izd-vo polit. literatury, 1942), cover 151

36. S. Ingulov, *Politgramota*, 3rd ed. (Moscow: Partizdat, 1934), 217 154

Acknowledgments

This study was begun in Moscow in 1996 during a research trip supported by the International Research and Exchanges Board (IREX) and completed between 2003 and 2007 with funding supplied by the Davis Center for Russian and Eurasian Studies at Harvard University and the Arts and Sciences Research Committee at the University of Richmond. Katia Dianina, Maya Turovskaya, Mark Lipovetskii, Jim von Geldern, Serhy Yekelchyk, Olga Velikanova, Peter Blitstein, and Bryan Wockley provided help at critical junctures, as did Terry Martin, Susan Gardos, Vladimir Brovkin, L. G. Zaiatueva, J. Arch Getty, Vicki Polansky, Natalya Panteleya, and George Fowler.

Terms and Acronyms

ACP(b)	All-Union Communist Party (Bolsheviks)
Agitprop	Central Committee Directorate of Agitation and Propaganda
anekdot	joke, riddle, anecdote
chastushka	traditional rhymed couplet
Comintern	Third Communist International
GULag	prison camp network
kolkhoznik	collective farm worker
komsomol	Communist Youth League
kulak	term of abuse for a better-off peasant
Cheka, GPU, OGPU, NKVD	various incarnations of the secret police
NEP	New Economic Policy, 1921–28
Nepman	independent entrepreneur during NEP
Politburo	Political Bureau of the Party's Central Committee
RSFSR	Russian Socialist Federation of Soviet Republics (after 1936, Russian Soviet Federation of Socialist Republics)
Sovnarkom	All-Union Council of Peoples' Commissars
Stakhanovite	honorific term for a champion worker or peasant

Introduction

At first glance, the idea that political humor existed under Stalin seems rather unlikely. What could there have been to joke about? Who, aside from a handful of party card-carrying cartoonists at *Pravda* and *Krokodil*, would have risked telling jokes in such a repressive state? Was political joking even imaginable within a country where everyone was supposedly "speaking Bolshevik" by the mid-1930s?[1]

Apparently it was. Although émigrés have long debated whether or not the USSR's distinctive culture of political humor dates back to the Stalin period,[2] broader interest in the subject has recently been stimulated by the discovery of political jokes in the former Soviet archives. Treated in passing in a number of studies,[3] the political humor of the 1930s and '40s takes center stage in this volume through the reprinting and translation of a rare collection of jokes compiled during the last years of Stalin's reign. More than merely a joke book, however, *Political Humor Under Stalin* also examines both the

---

[1] Stephen Kotkin, *Magnetic Mountain: Stalinism as a Civilization* (Berkeley: University of California Press, 1995), chap. 5; Jochen Hellbeck, "Fashioning the Stalinist Soul: The Diary of Stepan Podlubnyi (1931–1939)," *Jahrbücher für Geschichte Osteuropas* 44: 3 (1996): 371–72.

[2] Some testify to a vibrant culture of political joking, while others express skepticism — compare Dora Sturman, "Soviet Joking Matters: Six Leaders in Search of Character," *Survey* 28: 3 (1984): 204–08; and Zhanna Dolgopolova, "The Contrary World of the Anecdote," *Melbourne Slavonic Studies* 15 (1981): 1, 7.

[3] Early literature on the subject includes Eugene Lyons, "Red Laughter," in *Moscow Carousel* (New York: Alfred A. Knopf, 1935), 321–40; W. H. Chamberlin, "The 'Anecdote': Unrationed Soviet Humor," *Russian Review* 16: 1 (1957): 27–34. More recently, see Sheila Fitzpatrick, *Everyday Stalinism — Ordinary Life in Extraodinary Times: The Soviet 1930s* (New York: Oxford University Press, 1999), 3, 166, 183–85, 221; Sarah Davies, *Popular Opinion in Stalin's Russia: Terror, Propaganda and Dissent, 1934–1941* (Cambridge: Cambridge University Press, 1997), 28–29, 175–77, 185; James von Geldern and Richard Stites, eds., *Mass Culture in Soviet Russia: Tales, Poems, Songs, Movies, Plays and Folklore, 1917–1953* (Bloomington: Indiana University Press, 1995); Lesley Rimmel, "The Kirov Murder and Soviet Society: Propaganda and Public Opinion in Leningrad, 1934–1935" (Ph.D. diss., University of Pennsylvania, 1995); David Hoffmann, *Peasant Metropolis: Peasant Identities in Moscow, 1929–1941* (Ithaca, NY: Cornell University Press, 1994), 205; Robert Thurston, "Social Dimensions of Stalin's Rule: Humor and Terror in the USSR," *Journal of Social History* 24: 3 (1991): 541–62.

cultural context and the nature of the joking itself, providing a glimpse of everyday laughter and wit in one of the twentieth century's most authoritarian states. In some senses an archeology of Stalin-era popular culture, this study draws upon an array of diaries, memoirs, archival documents and interviews conducted with former Soviet citizens between 1950 and 1951 under the auspices of the Harvard Project on the Soviet Social System. It contends that humor in Stalinist society played an important role that has seldom been given the attention it deserves—as one Soviet diarist put it in 1933, "at some point in the future, when someone is given the difficult task of writing the history of our everyday life, it's difficult to imagine that he will be able to skirt the subject of political jokes." Continuing, this diarist explained the centrality of jokes and anecdotes to any understanding of the period:

> Within them, everything is captured in whimsical form: the ordinary citizen's hatred and protest against the cruelty and injustice of state policy; his hope and despair; his laughter and tears. Is there anything, anything at all, that hasn't made it into those jokes? They're openly swapped out-loud among drinking buddies while clinking glasses; they're whispered to one another while chuckling at intersections and tram stops; they're exchanged at work among colleagues while keeping a watchful eye out. Hope, despair, laughter and tears.... Sometimes these jokes are ribald or vulgar, but that only increases their appeal to the ordinary man, who's embittered enough to be driven to such things.[4]

Nearly twenty years later, one of this diarist's contemporaries echoed his sentiments, contending that "by studying the anecdotes, you can study the Soviet regime.... From a study of anecdotes, you can create the most correct picture of the Soviet Union."[5] Far from a laughing matter, then, political humor played a major role during the Stalin period that has too long remained at the margins of Soviet political, social, and cultural history.

Cultural Context

Most discussions of joke-telling under Stalin stress the degree to which the culture of political humor was governed by raw *chutzpah*. As is well known,

---

[4] Diary entry from July 24, 1933, in A. G. Man'kov, "Iz dnevnika riadovogo cheloveka," *Zvezda*, no. 5 (1994): 151.

[5] Harvard Project on the Soviet Social System (hereafter HPSSS), no. 149, schedule A, vol. 11, 42, 95 (idiosyncratic syntax is characteristic of this cycle of interviews; for other details concerning the HPSSS, see the Appendix). Emigrés still talked about the historical importance of Stalin-era jokes 35 years later—see Iulius Telesin, *101 izbrannyi sovetskii politicheskii anekdot* (Tenafly, NJ: Ermitazh, 1986), 8.

joke telling was considered "anti-Soviet agitation" by the secret police and prosecuted aggressively under Article 58/10 of the RSFSR Criminal Code.[6] Even so, political humor appears to have been quite widespread—some even claim that the majority of jokes told in the USSR during these years were of a political nature.[7] According to the memoirist Gennady Andreev-Khomiakov, "we knew there were NKVD informers among us, but we usually recognized and avoided them and they did not evoke much fear in us." He continues that although an unspoken taboo precluded joking around strangers, among "one's own," political humor served as a popular diversion:

> Scathing anti-Soviet jokes would spread through Moscow within a mere two to three days and be heard in the offices of Party executives and others, in homes, in shops and on the street. It seemed the all-powerful NKVD could not prevent this from happening. Never once did such an anecdote evoke indignation or revulsion in anyone. People merrily amused themselves at the expense of the authorities, … [reveling] in a common sentiment…. The Soviet citizen lived as citizens have always and everywhere, quietly gloating, chuckling, or bristling with indignation, giving the authorities "the finger in the pocket."[8]

Of course, the fact that many ordinary workers, peasants, and even party executives told jokes does not explain how the practice persisted despite police persecution. Memoirists like Andreev-Khomiakov suggest, however, that it was cliques, networks, and other unofficial social institutions—whether

---

[6] According to émigrés, sentences varied according to the joke. Poking fun at the Soviet government could earn a person three years, whereas jokes about Stalin were punishable with five years or more. See HPSSS, no. 30, schedule A, vol. 4, 17; also no. 32, schedule A, vol. 4, 54; no. 385, schedule A, vol. 19, 256; no. 512, schedule A, vol. 26, 24; no. 1296, schedule A, vol. 33, 31; no. 1498, schedule A, vol. 35, 17; no. 1693, schedule A, vol. 36, 12, 16; no. 1497, schedule A, vol. 5, 30; no. 1498, schedule A, vol. 35, 17. On Article 58/10, see Sarah Davies, "The Crime of 'Anti-Soviet Agitation' in the Soviet Union in the 1930s," *Cahier du monde russe* 39: 1–2 (1998): 149–68.

[7] Diary entry from July 24, 1933, in Man'kov, "Iz dnevnika riadovogo cheloveka," 151; Mikhail Boikov, *Liudi sovetskoi tiur'my*, vol. 1 (Buenos Aires: Seiatel', 1957), 359; HPSSS, no. 45, schedule A, vol. 4, 14; no. 79, schedule A, vol. 6, 8; no. 1582, schedule A, vol. 36, 10; no. 1693, schedule A, vol. 36, 62–63; no. 1705, schedule A, vol. 36, 45.

[8] Gennady Andreev-Khomiakov, *Bitter Waters: Life and Work in Stalin's Russia*, trans. Ann E. Healy (Boulder, CO: Westview, 1997), 131–32, originally published as *Gor'kie vody: Ocherki i rasskazy* (Frankfurt-am-Main: Posev, 1954). See also HPSSS, no. 127, schedule A, vol. 10, 36; no. 445, schedule A, vol. 22, 12; no. 1390, schedule A, vol. 33, 38.

FIGURE 1. Red Army soldiers

familial, professional, or patronage-based—that provided insiders with enough of a sense of security to make joking out-loud imaginable.[9] Perhaps the most common setting for this risky indulgence was at home among family members in an atmosphere that many appear to have believed was private and even privileged.[10] There, dissatisfaction with everyday life mounted into grumbling, sarcasm, and the exchange of caustic one-liners and wisecracks. Noting that "hard times and bad conditions forced families together," one former Soviet citizen explained to an interviewer in 1951 that the commonality of people's experience with "wants, needs, and sorrow" inclined them to try to make light of such drudgery. "We all had fun together, telling jokes and

---

[9] Theorists agree on the importance of the security afforded by such networks—see Mahadev Apte, *Humor and Laughter: An Anthropological Approach* (Ithaca, NY: Cornell University Press, 1985), 195. Some former Soviets confessed to having been afraid to take part in such conversations—see HPSSS, no. 1313, schedule A, vol. 33, 36, 64.

[10] Eugenia Ginzburg, *Into the Whirlwind* (London: Collins Harvill, 1989), 85; HPSSS, no. 445, schedule A, vol. 22, 12; no. 541, schedule A, vol. 28, 28.

FIGURE 2. Domestic scene

anecdotes against the regime," he claimed. "Joke telling got to be quite a pastime," functioning as a way of releasing pent-up tension and frustration.[11]

Although such dissembling seems to have been a feature of many ordinary households and family circles, it also found a place among the party elite. Indeed, one Soviet refugee claimed after the war that although all his brothers belonged to either the party or the Komsomol, "our parents cursed the regime freely in front of us." Apparently a common facet of everyday life, "anti-Soviet jokes were also told in the [extended] family. When a relative of mine who lived in Moscow came to visit us, he talked freely against the Soviet regime and brought us the latest anti-Soviet jokes."[12] A woman who grew up in relative privilege added that "from childhood on I was told never to tell outside home what mother and father said. And they always said things against the regime. When father came home from business trips, his friends

---

[11] HPSSS, no. 1240, schedule A, vol. 32, 44.
[12] HPSSS, no. 240, schedule A, vol. 14, 46.

FIGURE 3. Military academy cafeteria

always asked him: what goods did you bring back with you? For us he brought presents; for his friends, he brought jokes."[13]

This last comment suggests that while joking occurred at home, it took place in other contexts as well. Dozens of accounts speak of close friends and colleagues trading jokes back and forth on the street and in the workplace; some of the most daring even recorded examples of this political humor in diaries and notebooks.[14] Jokes circulated on the shop floor and in Red Army mess halls, in the corridors of public schools, academies and institutes, and even within the upper echelons of the party nomenklatura.[15] Of course, if joke telling was surprisingly widespread, it was also subject to a rigid set of social practices, as an interview transcript with a former jokester makes clear:

---

[13] HPSSS, no. 501, schedule A, vol. 25, 9–10.

[14] For mention of jokebooks, see HPSSS, no. 110, schedule A, vol. 8, 68; no. 127, schedule A, vol. 10, 36; no. 1123, schedule A, vol. 32, 10. A. N. Afinogenov mentions the compilation of such a jokebook in a December 14, 1936 diary entry at Rossiiskii gosudarstvennyi arkhiv literatury i iskusstv (RGALI) f. 2172, op. 1, d. 119, l. 265.

[15] HPSSS, no. 25s, schedule A, vol. 3, 15; no. 175, schedule A, vol. 13, 13; Andreev-Khomiakov, *Bitter Waters*, 131.

FIGURE 4. Industry executives after work

Question: In general, did people tell political jokes?
Answer: Yes, lots of them.
Question: To whom?
Answer: Oh, I could tell them to those I worked with. I knew them all. It was all a joke.
Question: Were there some people to whom you would not have told them?
Answer: Of course, to anybody whom I didn't know well... not under any circumstances.[16]

In other words, while political humor did play a role in Soviet society outside the home environment, this pastime was highly dependent on family-like bonds of trust and affinity.

Although joking on the domestic scene precipitated denunciations from time to time,[17] it was dissembling outside of the family circle that typically led to jokesters' downfall. Tens of thousands of Soviets were arrested every year during the 1930s for even the most innocent attempts at levity and humor. Scattered reports testify to occasional leniency on the part of the authorities— university students might only be expelled for a political joke instead of being formerly charged with anti-Soviet agitation, while Red Army soldiers might get away with an official reprimand or a dishonorable discharge.[18] Generally,

[16] HPSSS, no. 395, schedule A, vol. 20, 27.

[17] Ginzburg, *Into the Whirlwind*, 85.

[18] HPSSS, no. 424, schedule B, vol. 21, 17; no. 517, schedule A, vol. 26, 24.

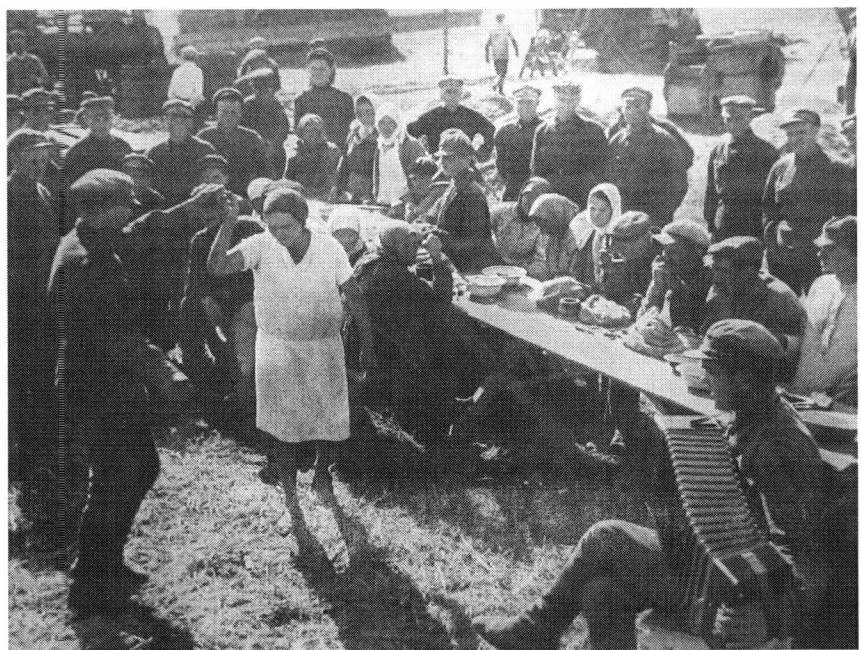

FIGURE 5. Celebration on a collective farm

however, party officials took a very dim view of the pastime. Widespread awareness of this punitive approach to political humor did not, however, discourage joke-telling so much as it encouraged jokesters to be selective about where and when they made their wisecracks.[19] Problems occurred when they failed to exercise sufficient caution, something that often came to pass in the context of social occasions where heavy drinking led to an unconscious lowering of inhibitions. Two former Soviet citizens interviewed in 1951 framed this peculiar sort of alcohol-induced candor by quoting the same proverb: "We Russians have a saying: 'Whatever a sober man has on his mind a drunk has on the tip of his tongue (*Chto u trezvogo na ume to u p'ianogo na iazyke*)."[20] Another supplied a story from personal experience that made the connection even more explicit:

> My uncle was arrested in 1931 for an anti-Soviet anecdote. He was an old man already, and he used to call on his friends [when he felt like a drink]. Once he narrated some anti-Communist anecdote. He did

[19] HPSS3, no. 1492, schedule A, vol. 34, 21; also no. 12, schedule A, vol. 2, 11; no. 25s, schedule A, vol. 3, 15; no. 395, schedule A, vol. 20, 27; no. 481, schedule A, vol. 24, 37–38.

[20] HPSS3, no. 483, schedule A, vol. 25, 18; no. 1664, schedule A, vol. 36, 13.

not know that among his former friends there was already a [police] spy. On the next day all of them were arrested and sentenced to 5 years.[21]

As this and other examples indicate, one's mere presence at such a gathering could result in arrest if someone in the group later informed the authorities.[22] A variety of motives precipitated such denunciations. Some betrayed their neighbors and acquaintances out of sincere, patriotic convictions, accepting the regime's equation of joke-telling with anti-Soviet agitation. Others went to the authorities after hearing someone tell a joke out of fear that inaction would implicate them in the crime as well. Personal jealousy and rivalries sometimes also played a role, especially in overcrowded communal apartments. Careerism explains still other cases, as people attempted to curry favor with the authorities by appearing fanatically vigilant. Indeed, some of the most infamous denunciations were penned by "professional" NKVD informers among the intelligentsia and professional classes—the so-called *sekretnye sotrudniki* or *seksoty*.[23]

If the threat of denunciation failed to curtail the circulation of political humor in Stalinist society, it did force Soviet citizens to develop a set of social practices that governed the pastime. Among other things, these rules tended to reinforce the distinction drawn between close personal confidantes and more casual acquaintances. As one man confessed to an interviewer in 1951:

> It is painful to admit, but people behaved like beasts. They fought for their security even if it was at the expense of their neighbors' lives. [One could] not trust anybody, unless it was a person whom one knew well for many years.... I had three friends with whom I played bridge for 20 years, and still we did not say everything that we thought, although our conversation was rather frank....

According to this informant, such a tendency to be perpetually on guard was critical for survival. After all, it was common knowledge that an ill-timed joke could result in many years of hard labor.[24] A former Red Army officer confirmed that among casual acquaintances, people "lived a life of pretense." Although he reported that he had been lucky enough to have a confidante

---

[21] HPSSS, no. 1241, schedule A, vol. 32, 20; also no. 1124, schedule A, vol. 32, 39.

[22] For more examples, see HPSSS, no. 481, schedule A, vol. 24, 37–38; no. 1011, schedule A, vol. 31, 37.

[23] Among those Stalinist insiders traditionally viewed as responsible for high-level denunciations were the court litterateurs P. A. Pavlenko and V. P. Stavskii.

[24] HPSSS, no. 1091, schedule A, vol. 31, 15. For a similar set of observations relating to student life, see no. 424, schedule B, vol. 21, 17.

FIGURE 6. Red Army soldiers fraternizing with collective farmers

with whom he could swap the occasional joke, the bonds he shared with this colleague were rare—indeed, only after "psychologically feeling him out" for several years was the officer able to conclude that the two "thought alike and could speak with each other frankly."[25] What's more, even the closest of such relationships were delicate arrangements that depended upon a host of outside factors. As one former Soviet citizen recounted, "when my girlfriend entered the Party, I could no longer tell her all that I thought." Not only was she "no longer able to laugh at anti-Soviet jokes," but now she felt obligated to report anyone else indulging in the pastime to the NKVD.[26] Other changes in professional and personal life, from promotions and demotions to the appearance of new colleagues, acquaintances, and neighbors, also affected the ease with which trusted friends shared anecdotes with one another. It's almost cliché to say that the key to telling a good joke is knowing one's audience, but Soviet citizens under Stalin took this principle very seriously.

---

[25] HPSS, no. 445, schedule A, vol. 22, 12.

[26] HPSS, no. 14, schedule A, vol. 2, 35.

Subject, Genre and Performance

If the contents of this volume are any indication, Stalin-era jokes were almost as diverse as they were widespread. Wisecracks about official ideology and propaganda alternated with those concerning more mundane, everyday issues; sharp tongues assailed both specific leaders and the system in general. Neither women and children nor ethnic minorities escaped unscathed. As one former jokester put it, there were "anecdotes that were political, anecdotes about local affairs, which usually concerned Jews, and then we had jokes about Armenians."[27] Few subjects were taboo—fear of secret police persecution failed to prevent wisecracking, even on the most sensitive of topics. According to one woman, "anecdotes were very frequent, on all political events. Even though one could go to jail for five years for telling a joke, people still told them."[28] Another man added that once the joking began, almost nothing was sacred: "I remember there were lots of jokes about the private lives, especially about [the] sexual life [sic], of high officials, including Kalinin, Mikoyan, etc. I used to tell them to the [local] Party secretary and he used to enjoy them. Of course, all these rumors and jokes spread like wildfire." Apparently only Stalin escaped sexual ridicule.[29]

Aside from a great variety of subjects and themes, there were several distinct genres as well. The most common jokes were often little more than caustic wisecracks, to be muttered under one's breath. These one-liners gave voice to dissatisfaction or frustration through the use of sarcasm, vulgarity, cheap shots and other sorts of disrespectful behavior and represent the most straightforward type of political humor under Stalin. Short and sweet, such wisecracks allowed jokesters to challenge authority while enjoying a degree of plausible deniability that more direct forms of public protest did not afford ("No-no, I didn't mean *that*—you've just misunderstood me....").

Gallows humor, a second, more elaborate genre of joke-telling, generally revolved around the bitter realities of everyday life. Drawing upon Eastern European traditions favoring irony, double-entendres, and self-deprecation, this was another strategy that allowed ordinary people to express themselves while minimizing their accountability for potentially unfavorable commen-

---

[27] HPSSS, no. 127, schedule A, vol. 10, 36.

[28] HPSSS, no. 1124, schedule A, vol. 32, 39. See also no. 446, schedule B, vol. 13, 72. Another informant noted that for most people, political humor consisted of exchanging "anecdotes in great number about the leaders; indeed it was a little dangerous to do this, because if we were discovered passing around these anecdotes .... we might have been arrested." HPSSS, no. 373, schedule A, vol. 19, 49.

[29] HPSSS, no. 1390, schedule A, vol. 33, 38.

tary.[30] Alexei Yurchak notes that audiences responded to this sardonic, self-reflexive genre of humor for several reasons. Most obviously, it played off of a universal fascination that people have with each other's foibles, idiosyncrasies, and character flaws. Reveling in the exposure of hypocrisy, this genre frequently juxtaposed the fraudulent claims of official ideology against people's willingness to live according to such lies.[31] As one female refugee recalled after the war, "Students used to make fun of the slogans and make up different ones.... [W]e used to add words or change words in the slogans." Through such provocative acts, ordinary people could reveal to each other the degree to which they "understood and cursed the propaganda" that defined their lives.[32]

Political humor's allure in such contexts was compounded by the jokes' deliberate violation of social taboos. Much like contemporary humor revolving around sexism, ethnic stereotypes, and racy subject matter, the jokes of the 1930s and '40s resonated with their audiences because their burlesque and satire provided a striking alternative to the political orthodoxy that dominated mainstream Soviet culture.[33] The most outrageous of the era's jokes—those told at the expense of the party leadership and Stalin himself—represent an extreme form of this sort of joking. A combination of disrespectful irreverence and the flagrant transgression of social taboo, this genre of political humor and its dogged persistence is perhaps the single most remarkable aspect of joke-telling under Stalin.

Perhaps unsurprisingly, the majority of the jokes told during the 1930s and '40s were bitter and dry rather than hilarious, jocular, or witty. For example, one classic joke begins: "For Marx, being (*bytie*) defines consciousness." It then immediately complements this ideological precept with the statement that "Soviet prisoners express this maxim differently, however: 'Beating (*bit'e*) defines consciousness.'" Ironic and self-reflexive, the humor here stems from the very structure of the joke. According to Yurchak, the first part of such jokes often focused on "a clichéd formula of official ideological

---

[30] Alan Dundes argues that such jokes serve as "socially sanctioned outlets for expressing taboo ideas and subjects." See his *Cracking Jokes: Studies of Sick Humor Cycles and Stereotypes* (Berkeley, CA: Ten Speed Press, 1987), vii.

[31] Alexei Yurchak, "The Cynical Reason of Late Socialism: Power, Pretense and the *Anekdot*," *Public Culture* 9 (1997): 178–80.

[32] HPSS3, no. 455, schedule A, vol. 23, 78.

[33] Yurchak, "The Cynical Reason of Late Socialism," 178–80. Yurchak bolsters his analysis with reference to C. Curco, "Some Observations on the Pragmatics of Humorous Interpretations: A Relevance Theoretic Approach," *Working Papers on Linguistics: Pragmatics* 7 (1995): 37, 47; and S. Freud, *Jokes and their Relation to the Unconscious*, vol. 8, *The Standard Edition of the Complete Psychological Works of Sigmund Freud*, trans. and ed. James Strachey (New York: W. W. Norton, 1960), 137. Arthur Koestler advances a similar argument in *The Act of Creation* (New York: Macmillan, 1964), 91.

discourse, which was repeated with a straight face (as if taken for granted)." This was then immediately followed by another statement subverting it, the joke's formulaic structure allowing the jokester to deadpan it in such a way as to distance himself from the official claim that he was invoking and then indicting. The end result, according to Yurchak, "attracted listeners' attention to the discrepancy between their own understanding and their behavior," producing a sense of amusement that was subversive and introspective without losing its mass appeal.[34]

Of course, the wry nature of Stalin-era jokes also stems from the repressiveness of the state itself. Humor generally evolves in complexity and sophistication through repetition in front of a variety of audiences, where word choice is refined along with timing and delivery. Under Stalin, however, common sense cautioned against the performative aspect of this process, leaving Soviet jokesters with few opportunities to fine-tune their craft. This, as much as anything else, explains why modern readers may find the era's political humor somewhat stilted and perhaps overly dependent on irony and sarcasm.

Stalin-Era Humor in Historical Perspective

During the late 1930s, M. M. Bakhtin identified carnivalesque behavior — everything from satire and joke-telling to public displays of vulgarity — as a subversive bid to liberate society from the grip of ideological domination.[35] But while Bakhtin may have been right that some Stalin-era jokes hint at conscious oppositional activity, the vast majority should probably be viewed as resistance to authority on a more instinctive, emotional level instead. Humor during these years generally functioned as an escape valve of sorts that allowed people to vent their frustrations without committing themselves to anything more than a passing expression of dissatisfaction with the status

---

[34] Yurchak, "The Cynical Reason of Late Socialism," 178–79.

[35] Although Bakhtin's work focused on Francois Rabelais' treatment of the tension between medieval society and the Catholic church, it is generally read as an allegorical critique of Soviet modernity as well. See M. M. Bakhtin, *Rabelais and His World*, trans. Helene Iswolsky (Cambridge: MIT Press, 1965); Katerina Clark and Michael Holquist, *Mikhail Bakhtin* (Cambridge: Harvard University Press, 1984), 295–320. Bakhtin's view was seconded during a postwar interview with a former Soviet citizen: HPSSS, no. 53, schedule B, vol. 1, 15. Many take an even more simplistic view of such jokes within oppressive political systems, seeing them as *a priori* evidence of articulate dissent — see Dundes, *Cracking Jokes*, vii, 159–68; Gregor Benton, "The Origin of the Political Joke," in *Humour in Society: Resistance and Control*, ed. Chris Powell and George E. C. Patton (New York: St. Martin's Press, 1988), 33–55, esp. 33–36; Robert Conquest, *The Great Terror: A Reassessment* (New York: Oxford University Press, 1990), 51; etc.

quo.[36] According to M. S. Petrovskii, such a sense of humor was highly personal and attempted to assuage "misfortune, humiliation and fright" rather than advance an explicit political agenda or undermine the established order.[37] Something akin to swearing and other types of disrespectful grumbling, joke-telling made a poor indicator of overall political loyalty—indeed, it was entirely possible during these years to make a wisecrack in private one moment and publicly swear allegiance to the USSR the next. Even when the jokes were daring enough to directly assail Stalin or other members of the party hierarchy, they probably had more in common with the limited, inarticulate resistance that the anthropologist James Scott describes in his book *Weapons of the Weak* (shirking, disobedience, verbal abuse, etc.) than they do with the mature and sophisticated political dissidence of the Brezhnev years.[38]

But if this joking was in many cases essentially devoid of lasting political and ideological meaning, memoirists like Andreev-Khomiakov certainly err in asserting that it never evoked popular indignation. As one former Soviet citizen recounted,

> I remember a banquet in honor of a movie director whom a cousin of mine had married. I was very gay, probably had too much to drink, and told two political jokes; the atmosphere became immediately strained and unpleasant. The whole party was spoiled.[39]

Choosing one's audience carefully was a serious matter—as the celebrated cases of O. E. Mandel'shtam and A. I. Solzhenitsyn make clear, even the naïve use of irony or sarcasm could be interpreted by party officials as an indication of disloyalty, if not outright anti-Soviet activity.[40]

---

[36] For passing treatment of this interpretation, see Yekelchyk, "No Laughing Matter," 80–81, Kotkin, *Magnetic Mountain*, 220; Davies, *Public Opinion in Stalin's Russia*, 177; Fitzpatrick, *Everyday Stalinism*, 186 n. 77; *Istoriia Sovetskoi Rossii (1917–1953) v anekdotakh*, ed. S. A. Shinkarchuk (St. Petersburg: Nestor, 2000), 5–8.

[37] M. S. Petrovskii, "Novyi anekdot znaesh'?" *Filosofskaia i sotsiologicheskaia mysl'*, no. 5 (1990): 49; more generally, Freud, *Jokes and their Relation to the Unconscious*, 102–15, 140–58, 233–35. For an extreme example of this phenomenon, see Steve Lipman, *Laughter in Hell: The Uses of Humor during the Holocaust* (Northvale, NJ: Jason Aronson, 1991).

[38] James Scott, *Weapons of the Weak: Everyday Forms of Peasant Resistance* (New Haven: Yale University Press, 1985), 29.

[39] HPSSS, no. 31, schedule A, vol. 4, 11. Many explained their caution in public by averring that the secret police had an agent in every bar listening for inappropriate jokes. See no. 34, schedule A, vol. 4, 13; also no. 96, schedule A, vol. 7, 41; no. 523, schedule A, vol. 27, 14.

[40] O. E. Mandel'shtam was arrested in 1934 for reciting an anti-Stalin epigram at Boris Pasternak's apartment among friends; A. I. Solzhenitsyn was arrested in February

Part of the reason that people like Mandel'shtam committed such indiscretions in the first place stemmed from the fact that political humor in the USSR had not always been considered counterrevolutionary. Indeed, party leaders had encouraged anti-establishment joke-telling before 1917 and tolerated it in the years that followed.[41] Efforts to suppress political humor date only to the late 1920s, when officials were told to stop turning a blind eye toward the pastime after the outset of the Cultural Revolution. In 1929, a leading party critic and artistic censor even proposed to rein in the humor found in officially-sanctioned Soviet literature and theatrical productions. The critic, V. I. Blium, justified his position by warning in *Literaturnaia gazeta* that "the prerevolutionary tradition of satire (aimed against state and society) is turning into a direct attack against our own state and society." Inasmuch as satire threatened to undermine popular faith in the system as a whole, Blium called for the genre to be banned from the stage and belle lettres and restricted in the future to journalistic accounts of minor scandals.[42] A reflection of the Cultural Revolution's radicalism and intolerance, Blium's reservations regarding satire were seconded by other artistic authorities.[43] *Literaturnaia gazeta* proposed a compromise later that year whereby the formerly broad, wide-ranging Russian classical tradition of satire would henceforth be redirected against narrow social ills such as superstition, religion, and nationalism.[44] The paper's failure to include perennial Soviet concerns in this list such as political orthodoxy, class consciousness, labor discipline, and cultural literacy indicates that such issues were now to be discussed only with the appropriate modicum of sobriety and reserve.

Resistance to this hardline stance among members of the creative intelligentsia like Il'ia Il'f, Evgenii Petrov, and V. V. Maiakovskii led to the staging of a public debate in early 1930 to resolve the issue. There, Blium rebuked his opponents, declaring that satire served only to provide a forum for hidden class enemies to attack the USSR. "We don't need satire," he declared. "It's harmful to our worker-peasant state." Such hyperbole enraged Maiakovskii and quickly caused the debate to descend into little more than a shouting

---

1945 for caustic commentary about Stalin in personal correspondence with his childhood friend N. D. Vitkevich.

[41] Note the neutral tone of the official definition of "political joke" during the mid-1920s: "an idiosyncratic (*svoeobraznoe*) political tool" that "acquires major agitational significance in moments of social crisis"—"Anekdot," in *Bol'shaia Sovetskaia entsiklopediia*, 66 vols. (Moscow: Sovetskaia entsiklopediia, 1926), 2: 744.

[42] V. Blium, "Vozroditsia li satira?" *Literaturnaia gazeta*, 27 May 1929, p. 2. Blium's broadside was a response to A. Lezhnev's "Na puti k vozrozhdeniiu satiry," *Literaturnaia gazeta*, 22 April 1929, p. 2.

[43] See, for instance, G. Iakubovskii, "O satire nashikh dnei," *Literaturnaia gazeta*, 8 July 1929, p. 3; M. Rogi, "Puti Sovetskoi satiry," *Literaturnaia gazeta*, 22 July 1929, p. 3.

[44] "O putiakh Sovetskoi satiry," *Literaturnaia gazeta*, 15 July 1929, p. 1.

match over the place of humor in Soviet mass culture. Although Blium was ultimately blamed for the fiasco, the satirists' victory was a pyrrhic one—indeed, even before the end of the debate, many of its participants had come to agree with Mikhail Kol'tsov that while Soviet satire had a right to exist, it also had a responsibility to uphold official state priorities.[45] This compromise, reaffirmed by Maksim Gor'kii in 1931 and again in 1934 by several speakers at the first conference of the Soviet Writers' Union,[46] effectively hobbled official Soviet satire at the same time that the secret police was attempting to curtail more run-of-the-mill joke-telling.[47] Fragmentary evidence suggests that this latter institution's campaign against political humor in society at large was aggressively enforced, leading to a massive increase in the number of ordinary people arrested on charges of "anti-Soviet agitation" between 1929 and 1931.[48]

Word traveled fast about the regime's determination to crack down on political humor—one diarist reported even before Blium's assault on satire that "the GPU has apparently been ordered to suppress jokes ridiculing Soviet power." Tellingly, however, the same diarist expressed doubts about the secret police's ability to stamp out the popular pastime, averring that "this folklore is not going to go quietly."[49] Evidence tends to confirm such suspicions, as the culture of political humor persisted despite its new-found notoriety. A good illustration is provided by events that unfolded in the wake

---

[45] Kol'tsov was the older brother of the famous Izvestiia cartoonist Boris Efimov. On the debate, see E. G. "Nuzhna li nam satira? Na dispute v Politekhnicheskom Muzee," Literaturnaia gazeta, 13 January 1930, p. 3; Efim Zozulia, "Fakticheskaia popravka," Literaturnaia gazeta, 13 January 1930, p. 3; Don Buzil'o [Il'f and Petrov], "Volshebnaia palka," Chudak, no. 2 (1930): 20; and archival materials published in E. Petrov, "Moi drug Il'f," Voprosy literatury, no. 1 (2001): 254–55. For A. M. Lunacharskii's 1931 attempt to revise views of the role of political humor under the old regime, see his "O smekhe," Literaturnyi kritik, no. 4 (1935): 3–9.

[46] M. Gor'kii, "Ob anekdotakh i—eshche koe o chem (okonchanie)," Izvestiia, 20 December 1931, p. 3; and speeches by M. Kol'tsov and N. Zarkhi at the first conference of the Soviet Writers' Union: Pervyi vsesoiuznyi s"ezd sovetskikh pisatelei, 1934: Stenograficheskii otchet (Moscow: Sovetskii pisatel', 1934), 222–23, 465–66.

[47] For grumbling about Blium's chilling effect on Soviet satire, see Bulgakov's famous March 28, 1930 letter to Stalin and several pseudonymous articles by Il'f and Petrov: M. A. Bulgakov, Dnevnik, Pis'ma, 1914–40 (Moscow: Sovremennyi pisatel', 1997), 226; Kholodnyi filosof, "Literaturnyi tramvai," Literaturnaia gazeta, 11 August 1932, p. 3; Kholodnyi filosof, "Listok iz al'boma," Literaturnaia gazeta, 23 March 1933, p. 2.

[48] Davies, "The Crime of 'Anti-Soviet Agitation,'" 150–51. Davies attributes the policy shift to the growth of mass resistance against collectivization.

[49] Diary entry from May 13, 1929, in I. I. Shitts, Dnevnik "Velikogo pereloma" (mart 1928–avgust 1931) (Paris: YMCA-Press, 1991), 115. The timing of this change is obliquely confirmed in the postwar interview of a university student at the time—see HPSSS, no. 1158, schedule B, vol. 22, 5.

of the murder of S. M. Kirov in December 1934. Never satisfactorily explained, the killing of this Leningrad party boss touched off a firestorm of political hysteria within the upper ranks of the party, where even the most powerful seem to have feared that a plot was underway to undermine the Soviet political system.[50] As the secret police struggled to expose what was assumed to be a mass conspiracy, their union-wide investigation of political unreliability uncovered instead an entire subculture of joke-telling and dissembling, much of it at least temporarily revolving around Kirov's sudden demise.[51] Mean-spirited gossips referred to the fallen party boss as a lecherous Casanova done in by a jealous husband and chided that he "shouldn't have been chasing other men's wives" (*pust' ne taskaetsia za chuzhimi babami*).[52] Scores of Soviet citizens—including party members—were denounced for trafficking in such disrespectful talk.[53] Others got away with it, like the vandal in a Moscow suburb who scrawled "he got what he deserved" under a portrait of the party boss in early 1935.[54]

Cheap shots and snarky humor concerned police officials because of their potential to provoke more threatening commentary. For instance, a Moscow worker who accepted the official story that the party boss had been assassinated was reported to the NKVD for speculating aloud that "killing Kirov wasn't enough; for something to happen, you'd have to kill four more."[55] The sudden death of a second party boss, V. V. Kuibyshev, only months later added fuel to the fire. Sardonic rumors that he had "died from eating too

---

[50] Leonid Nikolaev's motive for killing Kirov remains a mystery to the present day. His bitterness may have stemmed from his dismissal from a local institute; rumors of an affair between Kirov and Nikolaev's wife (who was the boss's personal secretary) have never been substantiated. See Alla Kirilina, *Rikoshet, ili skol'ko chelovek bylo ubito vystrelom v Smol'nom* (St. Petersburg: Znanie, 1993), 48–49, 104.

[51] See Tsentral'nyi gosudarstvennyi arkhiv istoriko-politicheskikh dokumentov g. Sankt-Peterburga (hereafter TsGAIPD SPb) f. 984, op. 5, d. 12, ll. 4, 16; f. 197, op. 1, d. 1008, ll. 11, 16; d. 873, l. 191, cited in Peter Konecny, *Builders and Deserters: Students, State and Community in Leningrad, 1917–1941* (Montreal: McGill University Press, 1999), 131; HPSSS, no. 395, schedule A, vol. 20, 48.

[52] This quip, as well as those following it, are drawn from two files in the former Central Party Archive containing correspondence from transportation-sector party organizations to the Central Committee on local political dissidence in the wake of the Kirov assassination. All date to February and March 1935. See Rossiiskii gosudarstvennyi arkhiv sotsial'no-politicheskoi istorii (hereafter RGASPI) f. 17, op. 120, dd. 174, 176, here d. 176, ll. 135; 20, 125. For more sarcastic comments about Kirov's private life, see Rimmel, "The Kirov Murder and Soviet Society," 58–63. For another example of high-ranking concern over political humor in Soviet society, see RGASPI f. 17, op. 120, d. 70, l. 58, etc.

[53] RGASPI f. 17, op. 120, d. 174, l. 68.

[54] RGASPI f. 17, op. 120, d. 176, l. 47.

[55] RGASPI f. 17, op. 120, d. 176, ll. 26–27. Also note d. 174, ll. 68.

much flour" were traced to a religious sect in Krasnograd,[56] while a worker in Khar'kov was fired for his heretical jest to a friend that "a spot's freed up on the Politburo—maybe you'd like to fill in?"[57] Party officials found such sentiments to be harbingers of widespread social unrest.

Needless to say, it is impossible to determine whether these snide and obnoxious one-liners were a sign of self-conscious and articulate political dissent or whether they were merely expressions of contempt and disrespect. Indeed, the only thing that is clear is that such nuances mattered very little to the secret police charged with reining in the popular pastime. Swamped with reports from Moscow to Saratov describing a veritable epidemic of joke-telling, USSR State Procurator I. A. Akulov declared the situation in 1935 to pose a direct threat to state security:

> In relation to the death of Kirov, an increase in the activity of anti-Soviet elements has been noted in the form of counter-revolutionary agitation, approving not only of the terrorist act against Kirov, but also of the execution of such acts against other leaders of the Party and Soviet government. This has given the procuracy the task of rapidly and decisively intersecting other types of counter-revolutionary speeches.[58]

Lackadaisical political mobilization, both in schools and on the shop floor, was blamed for the proliferation of political jokes; the police and court system were also reproached for being too lenient in their enforcement of the criminal code. Arrests quickly followed. A second-year technical school student named Pyrkov, for instance, was turned over to the police in Balakovo for telling the "most outrageously counterrevolutionary jokes."[59] Far away in Tadzhikistan, a certain Trofimov's sardonic connection of Kirov's murder with the end of bread rationing—"Kirov was killed and bread became cheaper; if Stalin is killed, things will get even better"—earned him a ten-year prison sentence.[60] Ultimately, the NKVD arrested some 43,686 people on charges of anti-Soviet agitation during 1935 alone,[61] over half of whom were accused of swapping jokes and couplets (*chastushki*), vandalizing portraits of party leaders or speculating about the fates of Kirov, Kuibyshev and other

---

[56] RGASPI f. 17, op. 120, d. 174, l. 112. For more examples of such audacious comments, see Rimmel, "The Kirov Murder and Soviet Society," 110–17.

[57] RGASPI f. 17, op. 120, d. 176, l. 158.

[58] Gosudarstvennyi arkhiv Rossiiskoi Federatsii (hereafter GARF) f. 8131, op. 28, d. 6, ll. 4–8, quoted in Davies, "The Crime of 'Anti-Soviet Agitation,'" 152.

[59] RGASPI f. 17, op. 120, d. 174, l. 71.

[60] RGASPI f. 17, op. 120, d. 174, l. 48.

[61] GARF f. 9401, op. 1, d. 4157, ll. 201–03, 205, cited in Davies, "The Crime of 'Anti-Soviet Agitation,'" 153.

Bolshevik bosses. Kulaks and other "usual suspects" were well-represented among such arrests, but so too were workers, peasants, and state employees.[62]

Perhaps unsurprisingly, this wave of arrests did not do much to discourage the circulation of political humor. In 1936, the Leningrad NKVD noted that problems were continuing: "at the Dentistry Institute, a student named Logicheva has been telling all sorts of anti-Soviet jokes. At the Zhdanov Factory, Fedorova, a former Komsomol member, is engaged in anti-Soviet propaganda. Not long ago, a notebook was confiscated from her that contained some 1500 jokes, a large portion of which were anti-Soviet."[63] Ultimately, about a quarter of all of those arrested by the NKVD for anti-Soviet agitation in 1936 were accused of joke-telling or making "terroristic" comments about the party leadership, while another twenty percent or so were charged with defacing portraits or making "counterrevolutionary" statements while drunk.[64] Reports from places like Khar'kov indicate that the trend did not diminish in the years that followed.[65] During 1937, some 234,301 people were arrested by the NKVD for anti-Soviet agitation, "a great army" of whom were apparently just "babblers," guilty only of telling political jokes out loud.[66] Despite this wave of repression, however, anecdotal accounts suggest that the culture of Soviet political humor survived the Great Terror intact; indeed, the USSR's signing of the ill-fated Molotov-Ribbentrop treaty with Nazi Germany in August 1939 quickly gave rise to an entirely new cycle of jokes.[67]

---

[62] A review of 473 cases that came before the USSR Supreme Court in September 1935 indicated that two-thirds concerned dissembling in regard to the Soviet leadership (46.5%) or unpopular state policies (26.8%), as well as other sorts of jokes and couplets (7%). Another 4.6% of the cases involved the vandalizing of official portraits. Of those convicted in the third quarter of 1935, 25.4% were workers, 24.3% were state employees, 13.9% were collective farmers and 32.5% were kulaks or uncollectivized peasants. See GARF f. 8131, op. 27, d. 73, ll. 228–35, cited in Davies, "The Crime of 'Anti-Soviet Agitation,'" 155–56.

[63] TsGAIPD SPb f. 598, op. 1, d. 5423, ll. 149, 185, cited in *Istoriia Sovetskoi Rossii (1917–1953) v anekdotakh*, 5. See also Rossiiskii gosudarstvennyi voennyi arkhiv f. 9, op. 29, d. 246, l. 1.

[64] Of the cases involving anti-Soviet agitation that went before the USSR Supreme Court in March 1936, 17% involved comments about the party leadership, 10% concerned joke-telling, 16% stemmed from drunken "counterrevolutionary" statements and 4% involved the defacing of portraits. See GARF f. 8131, op. 27, d. 73, ll. 228–35, cited in Davies, "The Crime of 'Anti-Soviet Agitation,'" 156.

[65] RGASPI f. 17, op. 120, d. 237, ll. 129–32.

[66] GARF f. 8131, op. 28, d. 6, ll. 4–8, cited in Davies, "The Crime of 'Anti-Soviet Agitation,'" 160; Ginzburg, *Into the Whirlwind*, 85.

[67] HPSSS, no. 30, schedule A, vol. 4, 25; no. 91/1124, schedule A, vol. 32, 39. Such wisecracks persisted throughout the Stalin period and into the "Thaw," as evident in V. A. Kozlov and S. V. Mironenko, eds., *58/10: Nadzornye proizvodstva prokuratury SSSR po*

Of course, political joking was not only a source of concern for the police. High-ranking party members repeatedly attempted to discourage the practice as well. Even before Kirov's murder, M. F. Shkiriatov beseeched his colleagues at a Central Committee Plenum in January 1933 not to underestimate the threat that political humor posed to the party:

> I would like to speak of another antiparty method of operation, namely the so-called jokes. What are these jokes? Jokes against the party constitute agitation against the party. Who among us Bolsheviks does not know how we fought against tsarism in the old days, how we told jokes in order to undermine the authority of the existing system? We know that all factional groups always resorted to such a method of malicious, hostile agitation. This has also been employed as a keen weapon against the Central Committee of the party.[68]

The frequency with which such warnings were repeated during the 1930s suggests that political humor proved difficult to suppress even within party ranks. At a Moscow conference in 1934, for instance, an official named Kirillov implored his colleagues to stamp out political joke-telling, reiterating that this age-old social custom could no longer be tolerated. "We often do not attach political significance to jokes and rumors," contended Kirillov. "But this is one of our enemies' broadcast frequencies. Anyone making such jokes, especially jokes referring to our party and our leaders, must not only be exposed, but dragged off to where he deserves."[69] This menacing statement was echoed in an internal memo written by a party official in Leningrad at about the same time. Condemning even the most innocent sorts of political humor, this communiqué contended that "jokes about the party leaders may gradually blunt revolutionary vigilance if they are treated in a conciliatory manner. There may be a Menshevik, a Trotskiite, or a class enemy lurking behind that joke."[70]

Such candor ultimately testifies to more than just intolerance within the party hierarchy. Apparently, the party leadership was concerned about the

---

delam ob antisovetskoi agitatsii i propaganda—annotirovannyi katalog, mart 1953–1991 (Moscow: "Demokratiia," 1999). A second volume in this series is expected to catalog anti-Soviet agitation cases between 1941 and 1953.

[68] RGASPI f. 17, op. 2, d. 511, l. 177, published in J. Arch Getty and Oleg V. Naumov, eds., *The Road to Terror: Stalin and the Self-Destruction of the Bolsheviks*, (New Haven: Yale University Press, 1999), 89.

[69] RGASPI f. 17, op. 120, d. 174, l. 146. For a somewhat more oblique statement in a published source, see L. M. Perchik, *Agitatsiia* (Moscow: Partizdat, 1937), 39.

[70] TsGAIPD SPb f. 24, op.5, d. 2678, l. 10, quoted in Davies, *Popular Opinion in Stalin's Russia*, 152–53.

fragility of Soviet society's foundational myths—particularly Stalin's cult of personality. The Stalin cult performed an important political function in the USSR during these years by casting the general secretary as the charismatic embodiment of the Soviet "experiment." Such an inspirational symbol was desperately needed in this fractious, multiethnic society—scholars since Max Weber have noted that charismatic leadership has the ability to unite polities that are otherwise poorly integrated or lack regularized administrative institutions. According to this theory, loyalty to specific leaders is powerful enough to mobilize fragmented societies even when there is little other patriotic sense of community or rule of law.[71] The Stalin cult performed precisely this function in the USSR, harnessing the power of the general secretary's charisma to bind together an otherwise motley collection of peoples, cultures, and territories. Ultimately, the unifying role of the cult in Soviet society explains much of the party's hysteria regarding political humor and other sorts of "anti-Soviet agitation," inasmuch as popular joking about Stalin threatened to deface no less than the central icon of party ideology.

All in all, the historical record suggests that there was a widespread but heavily persecuted subculture of political joke-telling in the USSR during the Stalin years. Caustic, ironic humor expressed individuals' disrespect for authority and functioned as a safety valve for venting social tensions. Although much of this activity appears to have lacked broader political or ideological motives, it nevertheless provoked a fierce reaction from the party hierarchy and secret police. These punitive measures are probably best understood as having been motivated by the fear that lampooning the party leadership would ultimately undermine the legitimacy of the Soviet system itself.

The present volume reproduces a broad selection of political jokes drawn from a virtually-unknown anthology published in 1951 under the title *The Kremlin and the People*.[72] Little is known about its compiler, Evgenii Andreevich, its publisher (apparently the anti-Communist Munich weekly *Golos*

[71] Max Weber, *Economy and Society: An Outline of Interpretive Sociology*, ed. Guenther Roth and Claus Wittich, vol. 3 (Berkeley: University of California Press, 1968), 1111–26; Immanuel Wallerstein, *Africa: The Politics of Independence—An Interpretation of Modern African History* (New York: Vintage Books, 1961), 99; Clifford Geertz, *Local Knowledge: Further Essays in Interpretive Anthropology* (New York: Basic Books, 1983), 121–48. In the words of one commentator, the cult served as a unifying mechanism at a time when "most of the components of civil society or of the modern state were missing: a reliable bureaucracy, a unitary, consistent notion of citizenship or polity ... or even a sense of psychological inclusion." See J. Arch Getty, "The Politics of Stalinism," in *The Stalin Phenomenon*, ed. Alec Nove (London: Weidenfeld and Nicolson, 1991), 119.

[72] *Kreml' i narod: Politicheskie anekdoty*, ed. E. Andreevich (Munich: [Golos naroda,] 1951).

naroda), or the S. Sliusarchuk typography where it was printed.[73] "Andre-evich" may even have been a pseudonym. As for the provenance of the jokes themselves, Andreevich writes in his preface to the original edition that he and his acquaintances heard "the overwhelming majority of these jokes while still in the USSR."[74] Others were likely collected among Soviet refugees in Central Europe after the war. Indeed, when a group of researchers for the Harvard Project on the Soviet Social System conducted interviews with former Soviet citizens in West Germany between 1950 and 1951, they were astonished by how many of their subjects remembered at least one or two political jokes from the interwar years. (For more on these interviews, see the Appendix.[75])

A militant anti-communist rather than a nonpartisan scholar, Andreevich was quite circumspect about the methodology that governed his selection of jokes. This should not preclude their informed use, however, as many consider such artifacts of popular culture to be important enough to trust even the most tendentious sources. Sheila Fitzpatrick, for instance, writes:

> Anonymous public exchanges on issues of the day, like those that occurred in every Soviet queue or railroad compartment, in markets, and in the kitchens of communal apartments, are the hardest of all types of communication for the historian to get at. Some Soviet ethnographers collected *chastushki* ... but the heavy censorship of the 1930s made it impossible to publish them without bowdlerizing them completely. We therefore have to rely mainly on contemporary NKVD "ethnography," based on listening in queues and markets and writing down the jokes and rumors, and the Russian popular memory, which is good for jokes even at half a century's remove....[76]

---

[73] Andreevich published political commentary in émigré newspapers like the West German *Posev* and New York *Novoe russkoe slovo* during the late 1940s. *Golos naroda* was a weekly paper published in Munich between 1950 and 1957 by the Union for the Struggle for the Liberation of the Peoples of Russia (*Soiuz bor'by za osvobozhdenie narodov Rossii*) and the Union of Fighters of the Liberation Movement (*Soiuz voinov osvobodi el'nogo dvizheniia*).

[74] *Kreml' i narod*, 5.

[75] During their interviews with over 300 former Soviet citizens, researchers with the Harvard Project on the Soviet Social System found nearly half their respondents able to talk at length about the culture of political humor in Stalinist society. This interest in the cultural aspect of the question stemmed in part from their concern over the authenticity of the jokes; there is even evidence that they attempted to distinguish between jokes heard in the USSR and those composed later on in Germany during and after the war. See HPSSS, no. 5, schedule A, vol. 1, 18; no. 20, schedule A, vol. 2, 39; no. 191, schedule A, vol. 14, 17; no. 446, schedule B, vol. 13, 74–75.

[76] Fitzpatrick, *Everday Stalinism*, 183. See also *Istoriia Sovetskoi Rossii (1917–1953) v anekdotakh*, 4.

Needless to say, the use of secret police sources or post-1953 memoir literature to reconstruct the culture of political humor in the 1930s is a rather problematic endeavor. Jokes collected by the NKVD may have been recorded out-of-context, transcribed incorrectly, or fabricated altogether by informers or the secret police themselves. Worse, this record-keeping—such as it was—was far from systematic. Despite Fitzpatrick's tongue-in-cheek description of NKVD information-gathering as "ethnography," it's not at all clear that the NKVD or the other security services ever attempted to collect a representative sample of the political humor in circulation at this time. In fact, the archives of the former USSR Procuracy contain directives issued in 1935 demanding that political jokes and other counterrevolutionary statements be stricken from all criminal indictments, trial transcripts, and sentences, lest these documents come to serve as new sources of humor for court clerks and other civilians.[77] Both incomplete and difficult to verify, the archival record probably presents as many riddles as it resolves.[78]

Collections published in recent decades that purport to contain Stalin-era jokes are unfortunately little better.[79] Indeed, despite scholars' enthusiasm for the reliability of popular memory, it would be wise to be a bit less sanguine about the possibilities presented by even the best of these volumes. Although a surprising number of the jokes contained in such collections harken back to Stalin-era antecedents, they are impossible to disentangle from the culture of political humor that accompanied destalinization and the Khrushchev thaw.[80] Among other things, their sophistication and polish testify to the increased tolerance and even acceptance that joke-tellers enjoyed in the decades follow-

---

[77] See the March 2, 1935 directives from the Procuracy and the Supreme Court at GARF f. 9474, op. 16, d. 76, l. 14; f. 8131, op. 28, d. 6, l. 31, cited in Davies, "The Crime of 'Anti-Soviet Agitation,'" 155, and the discussion of an August 15, 1935 NKVD order (#00321) in a June 26, 1936 letter from NKVD deputy chief Ia. Agranov to V. M. Molotov, at GARF f. 5446, op. 18a, d. 849, ll. 2–4. The author is grateful to Paul Hagenloh for the latter reference.

[78] The fact that Andreevich's jokes have been preserved in the original Russian make them more useful than others appearing in translation, whether in the periodical press (e.g., *Neue Zeitung, Reader's Digest, Catholic Review, Challenge*), memoirs (Lyons, *Moscow Carousel*), or even the voluminous Harvard Project on the Soviet Social System.

[79] See, for example, Dora Shturman and Sergei Tiktin, eds., *Sovetskiĭ soiuz v zerkale politicheskogo anekdota* (London: Overseas Publications Interchange, 1985; Jerusalem: Ekspress, 1987), 11–13; *Istoriia SSSR v anekdotakh, 1917–1992*; Iu. Borev, ed., *XX vek v predaniiakh i anekdotakh*, 3 vols. (Khar'kov: Folio, 1996); Bruce Adams, *Tiny Revolutions in Russia: Twentieth-Century Soviet and Russian History in Anecdotes* (New York: RoutledgeCurzon, 2005).

[80] Shinkarchuk shares this methodological concern—see *Istoriia Sovetskoi Rossii (1917–1953) v anekdotakh*, 4.

ing the end of the Stalin period.[81] Such jokes are better suited for characterizing how people under Khrushchev and Brezhnev remembered the Stalin years than they are for clarifying the nature of Stalin-era political humor itself.

These problems with archival and printed sources heighten the importance of Andreevich's collection, which was originally published during Stalin's lifetime on the basis of popular sources.[82] The present volume reproduces roughly two-thirds of the jokes contained in *The Kremlin and the People*,[83] organizing them into ten thematic chapters and laying them out in a split-face format alongside their translations. An arrangement usually reserved for scholarly editions of foreign-language poetry, this presentation preserves Andreevich's original Russian phraseology and lexicon while making the humor accessible to English-speaking audiences. This volume also cross-references Andreevich's jokes against variants found in other Stalin-era sources—particularly the 1950–51 Harvard Project on the Soviet Social System—inasmuch as this sort of triangulation can dispel even the most persistent doubts about the authenticity of the humor under discussion. Finally, this volume flanks Andreevich's jokes with nearly three dozen contemporary photographs and illustrations from long-forgotten Stalin-era publications in order to provide a glimpse of the propaganda that gave rise to such an extensive subculture.

As thorough as this volume's background research is, it is important to concede that further work on the subject still remains to be done. For instance, future investigations might continue to triangulate the contents of this volume against similar examples found in other sources. Connections might also be drawn both forward and backward in time—insofar as many recent Soviet

---

[81] On the post-Stalin period, see Yurchak, "The Cynical Reason of Late Socialism"; Anatolii Dmitriev, *Sotsiologiia politicheskogo iumora* (Moscow: Rosspen, 1998); Seth B. Graham, "An Analysis of the Russo-Soviet *Anekdot*" (Ph.D. diss., University of Pittsburgh, 2003). Graham's bibliography contains a vast collection of anthologies and criticism dating from the Khrushchev period to the late 1990s.

[82] The relatively late publication of Andreevich's collection distinguishes it from NEP-era émigré publications such as *Sovetskie anekdoty* (Berlin: Chuzhbina, [1928?]). For a discussion of such sources, see Rashit Iangirov, "Anekdoty s borodoi: materialy k istorii nepodtsenzurnogo sovetskogo fol'klora," *Novoe literaturnoe obozrenie* 33: 3 (1998): 155–74.

[83] Virtually all of Andreevich's jokes relating to the interwar period have been incorporated into this collection with the exception of those containing untranslatable double-entendres or prohibitively obscure cultural references. Fewer jokes relating to the wartime and early postwar period have been included, however, as many appear to have originated among Soviet refugees in emigration rather than within Soviet society itself. Most former Soviet citizens like Andreevich ended up in the West as a result of their wartime internment as Nazi prisoners-of-war or *Ostarbeiter* laborers; as such, their first-hand knowledge of Soviet society did not extend past the first few years of the war. See the introduction to chapter 10 for more on this methodological concern.

and post-Soviet jokes harken back to examples found in this collection, it stands to reason that some of the jokes assembled here may, in turn, stem from earlier revolutionary-era or even pre-revolutionary traditions. Other patterns of influence might also be explored. For example, did Stalin-era jokesters borrow from (or influence) official Soviet satirists' irreverent depiction of foreign and domestic enemies, bureaucrats and petty officials? Did ordinary jokesters seek out official satire journals like *Krokodil* and the cartoons of Boris Efimov and the Kukryniksy, or did their sense of humor evolve independently of mainstream Soviet culture?

Other lines of inquiry await investigation as well. How much did the demographic profile of Andreevich's informants in postwar West Germany influence the content of his collection? Was this volume's repertoire shaped by the fact that Russians and Ukrainians from European regions of the USSR outnumbered non-Russian ethnic groups and Russians from other regions? Would Russian-speakers from Vladivostok or Tashkent have told different jokes? Would Georgians, Uzbeks, and other non-Russian ethnic groups have possessed their own homegrown traditions of political humor?

Equally important are a number of issues surrounding the role that the non-Russian peoples—be they Armenians, Jews, or others—play in some of the jokes contained in this volume. Additional research might allow scholars to determine precisely what place ethnic humor occupied in a society that was at least ostensibly organized along class lines. Was ethnic humor a legacy of the old regime, or was it stimulated by aspects of Soviet nationality policy?[84] Was it a more or less innocent form of joking, or did it reflect emotions associated with chauvinism, Orientalism, or nativism?[85] Such research might also explain why Jews are portrayed so inconsistently in this volume. Some jokes cast Jews as clever tricksters or sardonic critics. Others characterize them as foreign interlopers pursuing careerist ambitions within the Communist Party. Still others cast Jews as sly "bourgeois" nepmen.[86] Would such jokes circulate together within a single social circle, or separately, depending

---

[84] Joseph Boskin and Joseph Dorinson, "Ethnic Humor: Subversion and Survival," *American Quarterly* 37: 1 (1985): 81–97.

[85] Among the Harvard Project's interviewees, opinions differed about the implications of ethnic humor. Some denied that such jokes betrayed chauvinistic sentiments, pointing out that Jews did not take offense at such jokes and even told them themselves. Others disagreed, one commenting that at first glance, it seemed as if "there was no anti-Semitism. But in reality there was a very deep anti-Semitism. There was also discrimination against Caucasians. One could tell it in the jokes that went the rounds." Compare HPSSS, no. 9, schedule A, vol. 1, 115; no. 127, schedule A, vol. 10, 36 with no. 1109, schedule A, vol. 32, 36; see also the diary entry from June 12, 1929, in Shitts, *Dnevnik "Velikogo pereloma,"* 123–24.

[86] These three categories resemble those outlined in C. Davies, "Jewish Jokes, Anti-Semitic Jokes and Hebredonian Jokes," in *Jewish Humor*, 2nd ed., ed. Avner Ziv (New Brunswick, NJ: Transaction Publishers, 1998), 75–98.

on the identity of the jokesters and their audiences? Should some be read as more or less anti-Semitic than others?

Questions also remain about the Stalin-era jokesters themselves. Further research might reveal more about who they were and how representative were they of *homo soveticus* as a whole. What made the jokesters more worrisome than other sorts of grumblers and complainers? What was it about the threat they posed that led them to be persecuted so much more ruthlessly in the USSR than in either Nazi Germany or Falangist Spain?[87] What were the precise rules that governed where and when might safely indulge in a bit of wit, irony or sarcasm? Were these rules uniform and consistent, or did they vary according to circumstance and milieu? And what other reasons might explain the stubborn persistence of underground political humor during this period, aside from the need to vent frustrations or express dissent? Did joke-telling provide a forum for asserting personal autonomy in an otherwise oppressive society?[88] Did it supply a way of negotiating social boundaries with acquaintances and friends?[89] Or was political humor under Stalin simply too risky an endeavor to allow for the development of practices and traditions considered normative in other societies?

Two final caveats of a technical nature would seem to be in order before proceeding to the collection itself. At times, liberties have been taken with the translations that follow in order to convey the essence of the humor and double-entendres into colloquial English. Minor editorial changes have also been made to some of the materials from the Harvard Project, insofar as they are drawn from hastily-drafted interview transcripts that were never intended for publication. Of course, even if it were possible to flawlessly render these jokes into English, many would still strike the modern reader as dry and sarcastic rather than uproarously amusing. A historical artifact of sorts, this bitterness should be seen as an intrinsic aspect of the political humor of the Stalin era.

---

[87] Rudolph Herzog, *Heil Hitler, Das Schwein ist Tot! Lachen Unter Hitler—Komik und Humor im Dritten Reich* (Berlin: Eichborn, 2006); F. K. M. Hillenbrand, *Underground Humour in Nazi Germany, 1933–1945* (London and New York: Routledge, 1995); Kathleen Stokker, *Folklore Fights the Nazis: Humor in Occupied Norway, 1940–1945* (Madison: University of Wisconsin Press, 1995); Oriol Pi-Sunyer, "Political Humor in a Dictatorial State: The Case of Spain," *Ethnohistory* 24: 2 (1977): 179–90.

[88] Lawrence W. Levine, *Black Culture and Black Consciousness: Afro-American Folk Thought from Slavery to Freedom* (New York: Oxford University Press, 1977), 298–366.

[89] Joan P. Emerson, "Negotiating the Serious Import of Humor," *Sociometry* 32: 2 (1969): 169–81.

Unofficial Jokes and Anecdotes

of the Stalin Era

The Revolution, Civil War and "War Communism"

In February 1917, the Romanov dynasty was swept from power by popular protest from below and elite intrigue from above. A series of clumsy and ineffective provisional governments followed—the infamous "dual power" arrangement—which accomplished little aside from compromising the credibility of liberal politicians and moderate socialists alike. Only the Bolsheviks retained their revolutionary credentials by refusing to participate in these temporary political alliances. As a result, by the time the Bolsheviks seized power in October 1917, they had become one of the most popular parties in revolutionary Russia.

Of course, consolidating power proved to be no easier for the Bolsheviks than for their rivals. Harkening back to the French Revolution of 1789, these Russian Jacobins saw the threat of counterrevolution everywhere. This was compounded in early 1918 by the collapse of an ad hoc Bolshevik coalition with other socialist radicals, which led Lenin and his entourage to become as nervous about the socialist left as the "bourgeois" right. By the end of that year, the Bolsheviks had been forced to resort to the use of political terror against their rivals, enforced by their own secret police organization, the Cheka. A civil war quickly ensued, which ravaged the lands of the former Russian empire until 1921.

These dramatic events are described in the political humor of the Stalin era in surprisingly vague terms, perhaps because many of the burning issues of the revolutionary period had faded from popular memory and disappeared from textbooks by the mid-1930s.[1] Defeated opponents were remembered only by their Bolshevik monikers (the "Whites"), while slogans like "Workers of the World, Unite!" had developed a largely cynical inflection. Memories of hunger in the cities between 1918 and 1921 were somewhat

---

[1] Traces of the political humor of the revolution, civil war, and 1920s are present in *Anekdoty pro tsaria Nikolaia dikaria na zlobu dnia* (Petrograd: n.p., 1918); "Sovetskie anekdoty," *Volia Rossii*, no. 2 (1925): 50–62; *Sovetskie anekdoty*; Shitts, *Dnevnik "Velikogo pereloma,"* passim; Lyons, *Moscow Carousel*, 321–40; S. Karachevtsev, ed., *Dlia nekuriashchikh! Anekdoty* (Riga: Kn-vo "Mir," [1931?]), 130–53; Nataliia Sokolova, "Strana moego detstva: Literaturno-teatral'nyi iumor 20-kh godov," *Voprosy literatury*, no. 4 (1995): 354–68; idem, "V zerkale smekha: Literaturno-teatral'nyi iumor pervoi poloviny 30-kh godov," *Voprosy literatury*, no. 3 (1996): 362–75; idem, "Iz starykh tetradei, 1935–1937," *Voprosy literatury*, no. 2 (1997): 345–64.

more vivid, particularly in regard to the collapse of communal services that accompanied the Bolsheviks' experiment with "War Communism." Most eye-catching is the fact that jokesters of the 1930s frequently described the party ranks in 1917 as dominated by outsiders—particularly Jews—undermining one of the most sacred myths surrounding the homegrown nature of the Russian revolution.

FIGURE 7. Lenin addressing a rally on Theater Square in Moscow

Оратор на митинге в 1917 году:
—Товарищи, 300 лет нам лили помои на голову, а мы молчали! Пора открыть рот!

A speaker declares at a rally in 1917:
—Comrades, for 300 years they've poured dishwater over our heads and we've remained silent. It's time to open our mouths![2]

---

[2] For a variant, see Karachevtsev, *Dlia nekuriashchikh*, 146.

Двое разговаривают:

—В революции в России виноваты евреи и велосипедисты.

—Почему велосипедисты?

Two people are talking on the street:

—Jews and bicyclists are to blame for the Russian revolution.

—Why the bicylists?[3]

☆ ☆ ☆

Комиссара спрашивают, какая разница между ЧК и ЦК.

«ЧК—это Чентральный Комитет, а ЦК—это Црезвычайная Комиссия».

A commissar is asked what the difference is between the ChK and the TsK.

—ChK is the Chentral Committee and TsK is the Tsecret Police.[4]

☆ ☆ ☆

Господь Бог заметил, что в России творится что-то неладное. Послали Исуса Христа выяснить, в чём дело. Проходит много времени—Иисус не возвращается. Господь посылает ангела разыскать Христа. Ангел возвращается с запиской:

«Ведут на допрос. Арестован. Христос».

Господь посылает на выручку Илью-Пророка. Тот также не возвращается. Посланный ангел снова приносит записку:

«Сижу и я. Пророк Илья».

Тогда, чтобы распутать всё это дело, Господь посылает Моисея. От того скоро приходит телеграмма:

«Жив, здоров. Нарком Петров».

God notices that all is not as it should be in Russia. He sends Jesus to determine what the matter is. A lot of time passes, but Jesus does not return. God sends an angel down to search for him and the angel returns with a note:

"I've been arrested and taken in for questioning. [Signed:] Christ."

God dispatches the prophet Elijah to help, but he doesn't return either. Instead, an angel comes back with a note:

"I've also been arrested. [Signed:] Elijah the Prophet."

God then dispatches Moses to sort everything out. A telegram is quickly received from him.

"I'm alive and well. [Signed:] People's Commissar Petrov."[5]

---

[3] Popular opinion assumed the Bolsheviks to be Jewish, as is clear from a related joke:

—Are there many Jews in the party?

—No, only about sixty percent.

—Who are the rest?

—Jewesses.

"Sovetskie anekdoty," 54; also *Sovetskie anekdoty*, 13.

[4] ChK, or Cheka, was an early acronym for the Soviet secret police, while TsK ("TseKa") was the abbreviation for the party's Central Committee. The humor here plays off the fact that in the popular mind, many commissars were Jewish and spoke Russian poorly or with a heavy accent. See HPSSS, no. 1011, schedule A, vol. 31, 45.

[5] Moses' use of the Russian-sounding pseudonym "Petrov" refers to the tendency among Jewish revolutionaries to adopt a Slavic *nom de guerre*. Lyons obliquely refers to this joke in *Moscow Carousel*, 338.

Еврей рассказывает знакомому:

—Мы с сыном Моисеем хорошо устроились: в Кремле на колокольне Ивана Великого стерегу зарю мировой революции, а Мойша служит негром в Коминтерне.

Знакомый:

—Ну, знаете, стеречь зарю мировой революции—это работа скучная....

—Зато вечная.

One Jew says to another:

—My son Moshe and I are doing pretty well. I'm a lookout in the Kremlin, keeping watch from the Ivan the Great Bell Tower for the dawn of the world revolution. Moshe serves [in blackface] in the Comintern as an African delegate.[6]

—Gosh, that must be a pretty boring position keeping watch for the dawn of the world revolution...

—Yes, but it's got the ultimate in job security.[7]

Двое знакомых встречаются:

—Откуда идёшь?

—Из Коммунхоза.

—А что в мешке?

—Заявки на дрова.

—А в другом?

—Ордера на дрова.

—А где же сами дрова?

—Да вот же, в сумке.

Two acquaintances meet on the street:

—Where are you coming from?

—From the Communal Supply Office.

—What's in the sack?

—My requests for wood vouchers.

—And in the other one?

—Wood vouchers.

—And where's the wood itself?

—Here, in this third bag.

☆ ☆ ☆

Мать с ребёнком прогуливается по парку. Навстречу им идёт мужчина в белом костюме. Ребёнок спрашивает:

—Мама, это белый?

—Да.

—А почему же его до сих пор не расстреляли?

A mother and child are strolling in a park. A man in a white suit is headed in their direction. The child asks:

—Mama, isn't that guy in a white outfit?

—Yes.

—Why hasn't he been shot yet?[8]

---

[6] The Third Communist International, a Moscow-based organization for coordinating communist movements abroad. Variant: "At a meeting of the Comintern: 'Khaim, rub some shoe polish onto your face—we need a speech from an African delegate.'" "Sovetskie anekdoty," 54; also *Sovetskie anekdoty*, 12.

[7] For variants, see Karachevtsev, *Dlia nekuriashchikh*, 132; Lyons, *Moscow Carousel*, 324–25; HPSSS, no. 628, schedule A, vol. 37, 21.

[8] Reference to the White Guards, a loose coalition of anti-Bolshevik forces during the 1918–21 civil war.

FIGURE 8. Communal cafeteria

В славные дни «военного коммунизма» в одной столовой общественного питания появилось объявление: «Сегодня мясные пирожки — рябчик пополам с кониной». Какой-то посетитель раскусил пирожок и требует завстоловой:

—Товарищ заведующий, тут рябчика и духа нет, где же пополам?!

—Пополам, так и есть: один рябчик, одна лошадь.

The following announcement appeared in a communal cafeteria during the glory days of "War Communism": "Today's meat pies are half grouse and half horsemeat." A patron takes a bite of pie and demands to see the head of the cafeteria.

—Comrade cafeteria director, there's not even a hint of grouse in here. Where's the half and half?

—It's half and half, as advertised: one grouse and one horse.[9]

---

[9] For a variant, see "Sovetskie anekdoty," 58; *Sovetskie anekdoty*, 58.

РСФСР

—Российская Социалистическая Федеративная Советская Республика
—Редкий Случай Феноменального Сумасшествия Рас
— С краю Розы, внутри Слёзы, а посредине Фига

RSFSR

—Russian Socialist Federative Soviet Republic
—The Rare Site of a Fabulously Stupid Race
—Roses on the outside, Sobbing on the inside and a Fig in the center[10]

УССР

—Украинская Социалистическая Советская Республика
—У-у-у, Сукины Сыны, Разбойники!

USSR

—Ukrainian Socialist Soviet Republic
—Ugh, Such SOBs and Robbers!

ВСНХ

—Высший Совет Народного Хозяйства.
—Воруй Смело Нет Хозяина.

SCNP

—Supreme Council for National Planning
—Steal 'Cause there are No Police[11]

КЕПО

—Киевское Единое Потребительское Общество
—Коммунисты Едят, Пролетарии Облизываются

KCCS

—Kiev's Co-operative Consumer Society
—Kommunists Chew, Commoners Salivate

---

[10] In Russian, a "fig" is an offensive gesture made by making a fist in such a way that the thumb sticks out between the index and middle fingers. A related joke deciphers SSSR (USSR) as "Shoot Stalin, Save Russia" (*Smert' Stalina spaset Rossiiu*). See HPSSS, no. 24, schedule A, vol. 3, 51; no. 102, schedule A, vol. 8, 40; no. 456, schedule A, vol. 23, 44.

[11] For variants, see HPSSS, no. 1498, schedule A, vol. 35, 17; "Sovetskie anekdoty," 53; *Sovetskie anekdoty*, 75.

The New Economic Policy

Often remembered nostalgically as "the calm before the storm," the New Economic Policy dates to Lenin's realization in 1921 that the Bolsheviks would have to find a *modus vivendi* with Soviet society in order to retain political power. In spite of the fact that the Bolsheviks had essentially won the civil war, almost seven years of conflict and internecine strife had wrecked the national economy, antagonized the peasantry and alienated many of the Bolsheviks' most loyal supporters within the industrial working class. Breaking with the radicalism of "War Communism," the party halted grain requisitioning in the countryside and legalized petty trade and manufacturing, apparently expecting market forces to ease tensions in society and restart the moribund economy. Perhaps the only thing more surprising than the Bolsheviks' willingness to indulge in such heresies is the dramatic effect that they had on the society: by 1926, the Soviet economy was enjoying levels of productivity not seen since 1913.

Although the Bolsheviks retained their monopoly over politics and the "commanding heights" of industry, the 1920s were remembered by jokesters under Stalin for their striking heterogeneity. *Déclassé* elites from the old regime rubbed shoulders with newly-enfranchised members of the industrial working class. Nepmen and other private entrepreneurs thrived despite harassment from tax inspectors and police agents from the GPU and NKVD. The party, too, "diversified" as it took over administrative tasks, shifting in the popular mind from a revolutionary vanguard to a ruling class, complete with petty graft and corruption. This impression of the wane of Bolshevik radicalism was bolstered by the party's apparent failure to make ideological inroads against long-standing traditions like popular religiosity. Particularly after Lenin's death in 1924, Soviet jokesters asserted that the October revolution had merely replaced one unpopular regime with another.

В «Правде» нет известий, в «Известиях» нет правды.

In *Pravda* (*The Truth*), there's no news and in *Izvestiia* (*The News*), there's no truth.[1]

---

[1] For variants, see HPSSS, no. 45, schedule A, vol. 4, 14; no. 95, schedule A, vol. 7, 29; no. 96, schedule A, vol. 7, 29; no. 302, schedule A, vol. 15, 29; no. 340, schedule A, vol. 18, 32; no. 451, schedule A, vol. 22, 42; no. 473, schedule A, vol. 24, 64; no. 1313, sched-

FIGURE 9. Lenin unveiling a monument to Marx and Engels

★ ★ ★

Старик-крестьянин, которому предложили подписаться на «Правду», ответил:
—Спасибо, сынок, я не курю.

When invited to subscribe to *Pravda*, an elderly peasant answered:
—No thank you, sonny, I don't smoke.[2]

★ ★ ★

Ленин сказал:
«Коммунизм = советская власть + электрификация»
Путём применения простейших правил алгебры, советские инженеры вывели что:

Lenin said:
"Communism = Soviet Power + electrification"
By using the most basic laws of algebra, Soviet engineers have deduced that:

---

ule A, vol. 33, 64; no. 1350, schedule A, vol. 33, 28; no. 1497, schedule A, vol. 35, 50; Sokolova, "Strana moego detstva," 357.

[2] Variant: "You know what the difference is between *Pravda* and *Izvestiia*? [...] *Pravda* has to be torn lengthwise and *Izvestiia* downwards to be rolled into cigarettes, that's the difference." See HPSSS, no. 7, schedule A, vol. 1, 3; also no. 1434, schedule A, vol. 34, 27; no. 1492, schedule A, vol. 34, 21.

Советская власть = коммунизм - электрификация

Электрификация = коммунизм - советская власть

Soviet Power = Communism - electrification

Electrification = Communism - Soviet Power

★ ★ ★

По случаю годовщины «Великой Октябрьской Революции» все советские учреждения и кружки самодеятельности ставили спектакли. Вот некоторые из них:

Текстильтрест поставил: «Где тонко, там и рвётся»

Финотдел — «Бешеные деньги»

Суд поставил «Без вины виноватые»

Театр им. Ленина — «Не в свои сани не садись»

Театр им. Сталина — «Каин»

Дом Кр.Армии им. Ворошилова «Недоросль»

Милиция — «Доходное место»

ГПУ днём — «Искатели жемчуга»

ГПУ вечером — «Братья-разбойники»

Наркомпрос — «Власть тьмы»

Совнарком — «Горе от ума»

Театр Пролетариата — «Бедность не порок»

Дом Крестьянина — «Живой труп»

Закрытый распределитель Кремля — «Пир во время чумы»

Кружки самодеятельности граждан — «Не так живи, как хочется»

Заключенные ГУЛАГ'а — «Мертвые души»

On the anniversary of the "Great October Revolution," all Soviet institutions and amateur groups put on performances. Here are a few of them:

The Textile Trust put on "Where It's Thin, It Tears"

The Finance Department did "Crazy Money"

The Court: "Guilt of the Innocents"

The Lenin Theater: "Mind Your Own Business."

The Stalin Theater: "Cain"

The Voroshilov Red Army Theater: "The Minor"

The Militia: "A Profitable Place"

GPU matinee: "The Pearl Fishers"

GPU evening: "The Robbers"

The Commissariat of Education: "The Power of Darkness"

The Council of People's Commissars: "Woe from Wit"

The Proletarian Theater: "Poverty is Not a Vice"

The Peasants' House: "Living Cadaver"

The Kremlin Grocery Store: "Feast in a Time of Plague"

An amateur group: "You Can't Live as You Please"

A group of GULag inmates: "Dead Souls"[3]

---

[3] Many of these titles refer to elements of the classical canon: "Where It's Thin, It Tears" (I. S. Turgenev); "Crazy Money" (A. N. Ostrovskii); "Guilt of the Innocents" (Ostrovskii); "Mind Your Own Business" (Ostrovskii); "Cain" (G. Byron); "The Minor" (D. I. Fonvizin); "A Profitable Place" (Ostrovskii); "The Pearl Fishers" (G. Bizet); "The Robbers" (F. Schiller); "The Power of Darkness" (L. N. Tolstoi); "Woe from Wit" (A. S. Griboedov); "Poverty is Not a Vice" (Ostrovskii); "Living Cadaver" (Tolstoi); "Feast in

Луначарский сказал как-то иностранным журналистам:

—Вы должны признать, что члены компартии обладают тремя достоинствами: они умны, честны и преданы партии.

—Это верно,—согласились журналисты,—но Вам придётся признать, что в каждом отдельном члене Вашей партии из этих трёх достоинств почему-то всегда имеются только два: если он умён и честен—он не предан партии, если честен и предан партии—он не умён, а если умён и предан партии—он нечестен.

Lunacharskii[4] once said to some foreign journalists:

—You'll have to admit that party members possess three virtues: they're smart, honest, and loyal.

The journalists reply:

—That's true, but you'll have to admit that for some reason, each party member has only two of these three traits. If he's smart and honest, he's not loyal; if he's honest and loyal, he's not smart; and if he's smart and loyal, he's not honest.

При приёме в партию кандидата спрашивает Комиссия:

—Принимали ли Вы раньше участие в бандах?

—Нет, никогда… это впервые.

A candidate party member is asked during his interview:

—Have you ever belonged to a criminal gang?

—No, never…. This is a first for me.

В К П (б):

—Всесоюзная коммунистическая партия (Большевиков)

—Воры, Казнокрады, Проститутки («б» в скобках поясняет последнее иностранное словоf)

A C P (b)

—All-Union Communist Party (Bolsheviks)

—All Criminals & Prostitutes (the "b" in parentheses—"bimbo"—clarifies the preceding foreign word)[5]

✯ ✯ ✯

Вопросы из анкет:

—Где вы учитесь, а если нет, то где преподаёте?

Questions found on all official forms:

—Where did you go to school, and if you didn't, where do you teach?

---

a Time of Plague" (A. S. Pushkin); "You Can't Live as You Please" (Ostrovskii); "Dead Souls" (N. V. Gogol). For variants, see Vlad. Azov, "Satira pod spudom," *Poslednie novosti*, 14 May 1932, p. 2; Sokolova, "V zerkale smekha," 374.

[4] A. V. Lunacharskii (1875–1933), the USSR's first commissar of education.

[5] After the start of collectivization, ACP was deciphered as "Again, Chains for the Peasantry" (*Vtoroe krepostnoe pravo*). Diary entry from October 22, 1929, in Shitts, *Dnevnik "Velikogo pereloma,"* 149.

—Были ли вы под судом и следствием, а если нет, то почему?

—Have you ever been on trial or under investigation, and if you haven't, why not?[6]

★ ★ ★

Один еврей долго рассматривал (впервые в жизни) верблюда в зоосаду и, наконец, воскликнул:

—Боже мой! И что большевики с конём сделали?!

A Jew was staring at a camel at the zoo for a long time, having never seen one before. He finally wonders aloud:

—What in God's name have the Bolsheviks done to that horse?![7]

★ ★ ★

В Москве один провинциальный еврей рассказывает знакомому:

—Мы здесь все хорошо устроились. Я теперь управляющий Сахаротрестом, мой Лёва—коммерческий директор большого завода, Сарочка заведует целым Наркоматом, Абрам….

Знакомый перебивает:

—А куда же вы всех русских девали?

—Русских?! Мы им купили мяч, они в футбол играют.

In Moscow, a Jew from the provinces tells one of his acquaintances:

—We've done pretty well here. I'm now director of the Sugar Trust, Lev is commercial director of a big factory, Sara is head of an entire People's Commissariat, Abraham is…

His acquaintance interrupts him:

—But what have you done with all the Russians?

—The Russians? Oh, we bought them a ball and they play soccer all day.

★ ★ ★

—Почему РКП переименована в ВКП?

—Потому, что большинство членов партии не выговаривают буквы Р.

—Why was the RCP renamed the ACP?

—Because most party members can't pronounce the letter "r."[8]

★ ★ ★

Провинциальный еврей приехал в Москву. Видит, в трамваях всюду давка, но с передней площадки некоторые

A Jew from the provinces arrives in Moscow. He sees that all the trams are crammed full of people, but that a few

---

[6] Variant: "They say that Point Number 20 of the Party membership application, which asks whether the applicant has ever been convicted of a crime, and if so, for what, will now be followed by a new Point 21, which asks if no, then why not?" *Sovetskie anekdoty*, 13.

[7] For variants, see "Sovetskie anekdoty," 53; *Sovetskie anekdoty*, 10.

[8] The Russian Communist Party was renamed the All-Union Community Party in 1924. The inability to roll one's "r" in Russian is a speech impediment often associated in the popular mind with Jews.

люди входят свободно, что-то говоря вожатому. Стал прислушиваться. Один, входя, говорит:

—ЦИК.

Другой:

—ВЦИК.

Третий:

—ВУЦИК.

Тогда еврей назвал своё имя:

—Ицик,

...и свободно вошел с передней площадки.

are able to get in to sit down from the front platform by saying a word or two to the conductor. He tries to catch what they are saying. One, getting on, says:

—TsIK[9]

Another:

—VTsIK[10]

Still another:

—VUTsIK[11]

So then the Jew says his name:

—Yitzik

...and is let into the tram.

☆　☆　☆

Жили-были трест и Меерович. Трест ничего не имел против Мееровича, Меерович ничего не имел против треста. Меерович начал работать в тресте. И опять трест не имел ничего против Мееровича. Меерович ничего не имел против треста. Трест не имел ничего против Мееровича, а Меерович имел против треста... собственный магазин.

Once upon a time, there was a Trust and there was Meerovich. The Trust didn't have anything against Meerovich and Meerovich didn't have anything against the Trust. Meerovich began to work at the Trust. And still the Trust didn't have anything against Meerovich and Meerovich didn't have anything against the Trust. [Things continued in much the same way:] the Trust didn't have anything against Meerovich, and Meerovich didn't have anything against the Trust... except his own store.[12]

☆　☆　☆

«Ленин умер, но дело его живёт».

Один армянин, прочитав этот лозунг сказал:

—Эх, Ленин, Ленин... лучше бы ты жил, а дело твоё померло.

"Lenin died, but his cause lives on."[13]

An Armenian, having read this slogan, said:

—Eh, Lenin, Lenin... it'd have been better if you had lived on and your cause had died.[14]

---

[9] Central Executive Committee.

[10] All-Union Central Executive Committee.

[11] All-Ukrainian Central Executive Committee.

[12] For a variant, see "Sovetskie anekdoty," 58; Karachevtsev, *Dlia nekuriashchikh*, 140–41.

[13] Party slogan popularized after Lenin's death in 1924.

[14] Variant: "A Stakhanovite went to Moscow to one of the conferences that are so frequently held there. As usual, he went to visit Lenin's mausoleum. That is where

FIGURE 10. Lenin Mausoleum (A. Shchusev, 1929–30)

Вскоре после погребения Ленина в мавзолее повредилась соседняя канализационная труба, и мавзолей залило нечистотами. Когда доложили об этом происшествии патриарху Тихону, тот изрёк: «По мощам и елей».

Shortly after Lenin was buried in the mausoleum, a pipe burst nearby and flooded the mausoleum with foul-smelling sewage. When Patriarch Tikhon was told about the accident, he declared: "Ashes to ashes, dust to dust."

Два еврея осматривают мавзолей Ленина, читают плакат: «Ленин освободил нас от цепей капитализма».

Two Jews were walking through the mausoleum and read a poster proclaiming: "Lenin freed us from the

everyone who goes to a conference in Moscow must go. Over the door there is a sign which says: 'Lenin has died but his work lives on.' The Stakhanovite read the sign and considered it for a while. Then he said 'It would have been better if his work had died and Lenin had lived on.'" HPSSS, no. 48, schedule A, vol. 5, 54.

Another variant: "Having emptied a Petersburg jeweler's store, some thieves left behind the following note: 'Lenin died, but his cause lives on.'" "Sovetskie anekdoty," 56; also *Sovetskie anekdoty*, 6, 76.

Один из них, указывая на свой живот:

—Вот и правда. Моисей, Вы помните, какая у меня была цепочка....

В это время к ним подходит милиционер:

—Граждане, отдайте последний долг и выходите.

Тот же еврей:

—Вы слышите, Моисей, мы же ему ещё и должны!

chains of capitalism." One of them, pointing down at his belly, says to the other:

—That's the truth. Moshe, don't you remember the nice chain that I used to keep my pocket watch on?

‣ Just then, a police officer comes up to them and says:

—Citizens, pay your last respects and move on.

—Moshe, did you hear that? He says we owe them even more![15]

Как известно, Крупская питала открытые симпатии к троцкистам и антипатию к Сталину. Опасаясь выступления Крупской после смерти Ленина, Сталин вызвал её к себе и сказал:

—Будышь партыю слушать, будышь вдавой Ленина. Нэ будышь партыю слушать, Артухыну зделаю вдавой Ленина

Everyone knows that Krupskaia[16] openly sympathized with the Trotskiites[17] and disliked Stalin. Nervous about what Krupskaia might say following Lenin's death, Stalin called her in and said (in heavily accented Russian):

—If you obey the party, you can be Lenin's widow. If you don't, I'll appoint Artiukhina[18] to be his widow.[19]

В Киеве пели:

Как хорошая хозяйка,
Нам была всем Чрезвычайка.
Утром рано мы здоровы.
А под вечер—на Садовой.

They sing in Kiev:

There's no host more generous,
Than the Cheka's been to us.
You'll feel one day as if your life's complete,
Only to be invited that evening to Sadovaia Street.[20]

---

[15] For a variant, see Lyons, *Moscow Carousel*, 338–39.

[16] N. K. Krupskaia (1869–1939), Lenin's widow and deputy commissar of education.

[17] Followers of L. D. Trotskii (1879–1940), a leftist ideologue expelled from the party in 1927 and the USSR in 1929. Assassinated in Mexico.

[18] A. V. Artiukhina (1889-1969), a well-known party activist rumored to be a favorite of Stalin's.

[19] The reference is to Stalin's use of his authority over hiring and firing within the party bureaucracy to consolidate power during the mid-to-late 1920s.

[20] The headquarters of the Soviet secret police in Kiev were located on Sadovaia Street.

☆ ☆ ☆

Партийный инспектор из Губкома заходит в Комбед в одной деревне. Его встречает председатель Комбеда, совершенно пьяный. Инспектор:

—Ну, как у вас тут дела?

—Ик... хороши... ик...

—Сокращается ли беднота?

—Так что... ик... вымирают понемножку...

—А с самогоном боретесь?

Председатель, протирая глаза:

—Значит... ик... весь уничтожаем....

A provincial party committee inspector pays a visit to a rural Committee of the Poor. He finds the chairman completely intoxicated.

The inspector asks:

—So, how are things going?

—Hic.... They're fine.... Hic....

—Are the ranks of the village poor contracting?

—Er, yes... they're dying off, alright.

—And how's the struggle with moonshine going?

Rubbing his eyes, the chairman replies:

—Hic.... We'll have it finished off real soon.

☆ ☆ ☆

Одно время во всех советских анкетах был вопрос: «Ваше отношение к советской власти». В первые советские годы люди давали разные ответы: «поддерживаю», «признаю», некоторые отваживались даже писать «не признаю». Позже все считали за лучшее писать «сочувствую». Этот ответ превратился в штамп.

Один армянин, подумав, написал так: «сочувствую, но ничем помочь не могу».

At one time, all Soviet forms contained the question "What's your attitude toward Soviet power?" At first, people gave all sorts of answers: "I support it," "I recognize it," and a few were even brave enough to say "I don't recognize it." Later, everyone decided that it was better to write "I'm a sympathizer." This answer became routine.

One day, an Armenian thought about the question and wrote: "I sympathize, but can't do anything about it."[21]

☆ ☆ ☆

На одном дипломатическом банкете, где впервые присутствовали советские представители, хозяин заметил, что с письменного стола исчезла золотая ручка с пером. Хозяин деликатно:

—Господа, я понимаю, что это чья-то шутка. Я сейчас погашу на одну минуту

At the first diplomatic function to include representatives of the USSR, the host notices that a gold fountain pen has gone missing from atop his desk. He announces tactfully:

—Gentlemen, I'm sure this is someone's idea of a joke. I'll turn out the

---

[21] For a variant, see Sokolova, "Iz starykh tetradei, 1935–1937," 349; also *Sovetskie anekdoty*, 12.

свет, и взявший ручку положит её обратно на стол.

Свет гаснет, через минуту снова зажигается, Все смотрят на стол.

Оттуда весь письменный прибор спёрли.

lights for a moment and whoever took the pen, please return it to my desk.

The lights are extinguished for a minute and then turned back on.

All eyes focus on the desk.

Where the inkwell and blotter have now gone missing as well.

☆ ☆ ☆

В обществе дипломатов зашёл спор о выдержке и стойкости дипломатов различных стран. Решили сделать опыт, кто больше выдержит взаперти в хлеве с козлом.

Первого пустили к козлу француза. Через пять минут он выскочил оттуда. Следующий англичанин выдержал 7 минут. Немец выдержал 12 минут. Наконец, впустили к козлу советского дипломата. Не прошло и двух минут, как распахивается дверь, и из хлева пулей вылетает… козёл.

A debate arose among some diplomats about the fortitude of their foreign service officers. They decided to conduct an experiment to see who could stand being locked in a pen with a goat the longest.

A Frenchman was the first to be shut in with the goat. Five minutes later, he jumped out of the pen.

An Englishman lasted seven minutes. A German diplomat lasted twelve minutes.

Finally, they shut a Soviet diplomat in with the goat. Only two minutes had gone by before the gate burst open and like a speeding bullet out shot… the goat.

☆ ☆ ☆

В Лиге Наций обсуждается вопрос о разоружении. После многочасовых дебатов, во время которых советский представитель как обычно предлагал «всеобщее разоружение», один делегат встаёт и суммирует свои впечатления следующей басней:

«Однажды на съезде животных обсуждался вопрос о разоружении. Лев, глядя на орла, требовал отмены крыльев. Орёл посмотрел на быка и потребовал запретить рога. Бык, обернувшись к тигру, требовал полного запрещения ногтей». Наконец, поднялся медведь. Он потребовал полного и всеобщего уничтожения всех средств нападения.

The League of Nations was discussing the subject of disarmament. After many hours of debate, during which the Soviet representative made his typical demand for "universal disarmament," one delegate stood up and summarized his impressions with the following tale:

"Once upon a time, a conference of animals took up the question of disarmament. The lion, looking at the eagle, demanded a ban on wings. The eagle, looking at the bull, demanded a ban on horns. The bull, looking at the tiger, demanded a total ban on claws. Finally, the bear rose to speak. He demanded a complete and total ban on every sort of weapon. But don't you think

Не для того ли, чтобы он смог захватить в свои лапы всех?»

he did this so that he'd be able to snatch everyone up into a big bear hug?"

⭐ ⭐ ⭐

Мальчик, гуляя с матерью, замечает священника с крестом на груди:
—Мама, кто это? Учитель арифметики?

A little boy out for a walk with his mother sees a priest with a cross hanging around his neck.
—Mama, who's that? A math teacher?

⭐ ⭐ ⭐

На курсах подготовки домработниц их просвещают главным образом насчёт «религиозных предрассудков»: Бога нет, религия—это опиум для народа и т.п. По окончании курсов устраивается выпускной экзамен. После экзамена одна работница с дрожью в голосе спрашивает:
—Начальник, милый, чи я выдержала?
—Ты?—смотрит в список— Выдержала.
—Ну, слава Богу. Я три дня из церкви не выходила, поклоны била за это самое....

In housekeeper-training courses, most of the instruction revolved around "religious superstition": there's no such thing as God, religion is the opiate of the masses, etc. Each course ended with final exams. After one such exam, a housekeeper asks her teacher with a shaky voice:
—Excuse me, comrade, did I pass?
—You?—he looks at his list—Yes, you passed.
—Thank God! I've been praying so hard I haven't left church for three days....

⭐ ⭐ ⭐

Комсомолец обращается к старушке:
—Как живётся, бабушка?
—Слава Богу, хорошо.
—Бога нет, бабуся.
—Так, так... а чёрта?
—И чёрта нет.
—А кто же тогда вас принёс на нашу голову?!

A member of the Komsomol[22] asks an old woman:
—How are you doing, granny?
—Fine, thank God.
—There is no God, granny.
—Hmm. What about the devil?
—There's no devil either.
—Well who saddled us with you, then?

⭐ ⭐ ⭐

Дворяне произошли от Адама, а хамы—от Дарвина.

The nobles came from Adam, and the rabble from Darwin.

---

[22] Communist Youth League.

Знаменитый физиолог академик Павлов был человеком религиозным. Проходя мимо церкви, он снял шапку и перекрестился. Какой-то комсомолец подошел сзади, положил ему руку на плечо и вздохнул:

—Темнота, дедушка, темнота.

The famous physiologist Academician Pavlov was a religious person. One day, while passing by a church, he took off his hat and crossed himself. A Komsomol member came up to him from behind, put a hand on his shoulder, and sighed:

—You're so ignorant, granddad, so ignorant.[23]

☆ ☆ ☆

Первая советская водка «рыковка» была 42-градусная, тогда как водка царского времени была 40 градусов. Был тогда дух НЭПа, и люди говорили:

—И стоило из-за 2 градусов революцию делать?!

"Rykovka," the first NEP-era Soviet vodka, was 84 proof, while tsarist-era vodka was only 80 proof.[24] People grumbled:

—Was the revolution really worth having for only 4 extra proof?

☆ ☆ ☆

Старушка, увидев длинный ряд остановившихся трамваев:

—Боже мой, до чего мы дожили! Даже трамваи в очередь становятся!

An old woman catches sight of a long row of trams:

—My God, look what things have come to. Even the trams are standing in line!

☆ ☆ ☆

В Америке в цирке атлет выжимает в кулаке лимон и предлагает тому, кто сможет выжать хоть каплю, 500 долларов.

Из публики выскакивает невзрачный человек, выбегает на арену, быстро выжимает две капли и говорит:

—Разрешите получить 1000 долларов.

A strongman in an American circus squeezes a lemon in his fist and then offers $500 to anyone from the audience who can wring even a single drop from it. A nondescript man jumps up, runs down the aisle into the arena, and quickly squeezes two drops of juice out of the lemon. He says:

—There you go. $1000 please.

---

[23] Variant: "Have you heard that Pavlov had his own church, which was built especially for him? And do you know that story about the Pioneer who saw Pavlov coming out of the church and said to him 'Oh darkness, darkness' (*temnota*)." HPSSS, no. 96, schedule A, vol. 7, 19; also no. 628, schedule A, vol. 29, 27; no. 1693, schedule A, vol. 36, 28.

[24] Here Andreevich evidently misremembers that the first Soviet vodka—named after A. I. Rykov (1881–1938), an Old Bolshevik and early Soviet head of state—was only 60 proof instead of the traditional 80. See variants in diary entries from December 20 and 29, 1924 and January 2, 1925, in Bulgakov, *Dnevnik, Pis'ma, 1914–1940*, 73, 81–82.

Все поражены.
Атлет дрожащим голосом:
—Кто Вы, сэр?
—Фининспектор из СССР.

Everyone's amazed.
With a trembling voice, the strongman asks him:
—Sir, who are you?
—A Soviet tax inspector.

Арестованного еврея НЭПмана спрашивают:
—Ваше отношение к Советской власти?
—Я, собственно, со всем согласен. Если и есть расхождения, то только по двум вопросам....
—По каким?
—По транспортному и по земельному.
—Так. Какие же расхождения?
—Советская власть хочет, чтобы я ехал в Соловки, а я хотел бы, чтобы она туда поехала. Потом, власть хочет меня загнать в землю, а я хотел бы её туда загнать.

A Jewish Nepman[25] is asked after his arrest:
—What is your relationship to Soviet power?
—I agree with everything. If I have any disagreements, they're confined to two issues.
—Which ones?
—Transport and land use.
—Okay. What are the disagreements?
—Soviet power would like to send me to Solovki[26] and I would like to send Soviet power there instead. Soviet power would like to bury me and I'd also like to see Soviet power six feet under.[27]

В тюрьме ГПУ НЭПманы беседуют:
—Рабинович, а что Вы будете делать, если Вас сошлют в Нарым?
—Поверьте, я и там не пропаду: сначала я повернусь «лицом к деревне» и буду скупать пушнину, а потом я повернусь «лицом к городу» и буду её продавать.

Two Nepmen are talking in a GPU prison:
—Rabinovich, what will you do if you're sent to Narym?[28]
—I won't let Narym be the end of me. First I'll "face the village" and buy up lots of fur, and them I'll "face the city" and sell it there.[29]

---

[25] Petty merchants, traders, and manufacturers during the New Economic Policy. Jews were believed to be over-represented within the ranks of these "bourgeois elements."

[26] A GULag camp in the far north on the Solovetskii islands.

[27] This joke was adapted to describe the relationship between fascists and communists after the signing of the 1939 Molotov-Ribbentrop treaty—see p. 123–24.

[28] A barren region in the far north where Soviet authorities exiled class enemies.

[29] "Face the Village" and "Face the City" were campaigns which called upon party and state officials to address everyday concerns among rural and urban populations.

На службе:
—А почему нет сегодня Александрова на работе?
—Ночью он заболел «золотухой».

At work:
—Why isn't Aleksandrov here today?
—Last night he came down with "yellow fever."[30]

Следователь ГПУ увещевает арестованного:
—Вы всё-таки не хотите отдать нам Ваше золото, Меерович. Поймите, что оно нужно для построения социализма. Подите [sic, Пойдите] в вашу камеру и подумайте.
На следующий день следователь спрашивает:
—Ну, как? Подумали Вы, о чём мы вчера говорили?
—Подумал: по-моему, зачем строить социализм, если его не на что строить....

A GPU investigator asks an arrested man:
—Meerovich, do you still refuse to surrender your gold? Don't you understand that it's necessary for the construction of socialism? Go back to your cell and think about it.
The next day, the inspector asks him:
—Well, did you think about what we talked about last night?
—Yes, and I was wondering why you decided to build socialism if you knew you didn't have the money to do it....

В 1927 году СССР посетил падишах Афганистана Амманула-хан. Сталин принимал его со всеми восточными почестями: с ковровыми дорожками, разостланными от поезда до автомобиля, с подношениями и с соблюдением обычая дарить гостю всякую вещь, которая ему понравится. Когда Амманула-хан уехал, спрашивали:
—Какое одно единственное русское слово выучил Амманула-хан?
—«Заверните».

In 1927, Khan Ammanula of Afghanistan visited the USSR.[31] Stalin received him with all the appropriate eastern honors. A red carpet stretched from his train car to his limousine, and as was the custom, he was given whatever he wanted as a gift. When Khan Ammanula left, people joked:
— What was the only Russian expression that Khan Ammanula mastered during his stay?"
—"Wrap this up, please."

---

[30] A colloquial way of saying that he had been arrested for possession of gold bullion. Nepmen possessing gold or other valuables were sometimes picked up and held in detention to coerce them into surrendering their assets.

[31] Khan Ammanula's visit to the USSR took place in April–May 1928.

FIGURE 11. S. M. Budennyi

Советский писатель Бабель написал пропагандистскую книгу «Первая конная» про армию Будёного. У последнего спрашивают:

—Семён Михайлович, Вам нравится Бабель?

Будёный, покручивая усы:

—Хм…. Смотря какая.

The Soviet writer Isaac Babel' wrote a propagandistic book about Budennyi's army entitled *Red Cavalry.* The latter was asked:

—Semen Mikhailovich, what do you think of Babel'?

Budennyi,[32] twirling his mustache, replied:

—Hmmm, that depends… is she my type?[33]

В 1928 году, во время поисков потерпевшего крушение итальянского полярника Нобиле, на почтах СССР было сделано распоряжение

During the 1928 search for Nobile,[34] a stranded Italian polar explorer, it was decreed that the Soviet postal service would deliver any correspondence

---

[32] S. M. Budennyi (1883–1973), a Soviet marshal and civil war hero.

[33] In Russian, Babel' sounds a lot like *baba,* the word for "broad" or "hussy." Budennyi's failure to recognize the writer's name is unlikely, of course, as Babel's unflattering description of Budennyi's unit earned him the commander's lasting enmity.

[34] Umberto Nobile (1885–1978), an Italian aeronautical engineer and Arctic explorer whose airship Italia crashed en route to the North Pole in 1928.

concerning the search free of charge. A Jew in Odessa sends a telegram to his friend in Moscow:

—Abramovich, save Nobile; if that fails, send me 40 sacks of sugar.[35]

A homeless orphan with a cold is coughing. Someone asks him:

—What's the matter, little fellow?

The orphan replies gravely:

—Lenin died, Dzerzhinskii[36] passed away, and now I'm not feeling very well.

During negotiations with American representatives concerning a loan for the USSR, the Americans ask:

—What sort of guarantee can you offer?

—Coal, iron, and gold.

—But that's all buried underground. What do you have on hand that you can offer?

The USSR's representative replies with exaggerated pride:

—The Soviet government.

After thinking for a moment, the Americans say:

—We'll give you the loan... when your coal, iron, and gold are on hand and your "government" is six feet under.

---

[35] For variants, see the diary entry from July 10, 1928 in Shitts, *Dnevnik "Velikogo pereloma,"* 40; Sokolova, "Strana moego detstva," 361.

[36] F. E. Dzerzhinskii (1877–1926), the first head of the Soviet secret police, was credited with efforts to set up early orphanage networks.

Stalin's Revolution from Above

Toward the end of the 1920s, the party signaled that the exigencies of the NEP era had come to an end and that it was time for the construction of "socialism in one country" to proceed as planned. Struggling with popular doubts about his status as Lenin's successor, Stalin used his power within the central bureaucracy to outflank the party's left wing—first L. D. Trotskii and then L. B. Kamenev and G. E. Zinov'ev. Once their defeat was ensured, he turned on his erstwhile rightist allies N. I. Bukharin and A. I. Rykov as soon as the opportunity presented itself.

Even before the final rout of the left and right, Stalin and his entourage broke with the liberalism of NEP between 1927 and 1928 in order to launch the first Five-Year Plan under the supervision of a central Gosplan bureaucracy. Political humor of the era recalled this new regimentation of the economy as precipitating a massive shortage of basic consumer goods. This supply crisis, in turn, resulted in a veritable public relations disaster, inasmuch as the party was attempting to restore a sense of revolutionary idealism to the Soviet "experiment" by rationalizing the economy and purging it of all vestiges of "bourgeois" corruption from the NEP era. Further radicalism was the result.

Затравленному сталинским «аппаратом» Троцкому было предложено публично заявить: «Сталин–вождь мировой революции», и извиниться.

Троцкий подчинился и заявил на партсъезде: «Сталин–вождь мировой революции?? Извиняюсь!!!»

After being hounded by Stalin's bureaucratic "machine," Trotskii was given a chance to apologize and publicly acknowledge that Stalin was the leader of the world revolution.

Trotskii agreed and announced at a party congress: "Stalin is the leader of the world revolution?? I'm so sorry!"

★ ★ ★

В Политбюро была получена покаянная телеграмма Троцкого. Калинин зачитал её так:

The Politburo received a repentent telegram from Trotskii. Kalinin[1] reads it aloud:

---

[1] M. I. Kalinin (1875–1946), an Old Bolshevik and nominal Soviet head of state whose peasant roots and advanced age made him the butt of many jokes.

FIGURE 12. K. E. Voroshilov

—«Я ошибался, а вы–нет. Вы были правы, а я—нет. Лев Троцкий».

Члены Политбюро уже готовы были аплодировать, как вдруг Каганович вскочил:

—Вы же неправильно поняли телеграмму, дайте-ка я её прочитаю! «Я ошибался, а вы– нет? Вы были правы, а я—нет? Лев Троцкий.»

—"I made mistakes and you didn't. You were right and I was wrong. [Signed:] Lev Trotskii."

The members of the Politburo are about to applaud when Kaganovich[2] jumps to his feet:

—You've read the telegram incorrectly—let me read it. "I made mistakes and you didn't? You were right and I was wrong? [Signed:] Lev Trotskii."[3]

Клим Ворошилов обвинял Радека в том, что тот «плетётся в хвосте у Льва Троцкого».

На это Радек ответил:

Не варит Клима голова,

И мозг его—развалина.

Klim Voroshilov[4] accused Radek[5] of "wagging about like Trotskii's tail."

Radek answered:

Voroshilov can hardly think,

His brains must be on the blink.

---

[2] L. M. Kaganovich (1893–1991), one of Stalin's most powerful deputies in the Politburo.

[3] The confusion stems from the fact that telegrams do not include punctuation marks.

[4] K. E. Voroshilov (1881–1961), an Old Bolshevik, Red Army commander and close associate of Stalin.

[5] K. B. Radek (1885–1939), a leftist Old Bolshevik known for his independence, wit, and frustration with Stalin.

Лучше быть хвостом у Льва,
Чем ж... у Сталина.

It's better to be Trotskii's tail, I'd say
Than kiss Stalin's ass all day![6]

☆ ☆ ☆

Когда в партии появилось «левое крыло» (троцкисты), а за ним «правое» (бухаринцы), один беспартийный спросил по-дружески у видного коммуниста:

—Теперь уже у вас два крыла, так почему же вы не летите к чёртовой матери?

When the party turned out to have a "left wing" (the Trotskiites) and a "right wing" (the Bukharinites[7]), a non-party member asked a prominent communist jokingly:

—Now that you have those two wings, why don't you all take a flying leap?

☆ ☆ ☆

Армянина спрашивают кто такой Сталин? Он отвечает:

—Маркса знаешь?

—Слыхал.

—А Ленина знаешь?

—Тоже слыхал.

—Так вот: ни на того, ни на другого нэ пахожий.

Someone asks an Armenian who Stalin is. He answers (in heavily accented Russian):

—Do you know who Marx is?

—Yes, I've heard.

—And do you know who Lenin is?

—Yes, I've heard.

—Okay, so Stalin's nothing like either of them.

☆ ☆ ☆

Загадка:
Почему Ленин ходил в ботинках, а Сталин —всегда в сапогах?

Отгадка:
Потому, что Ленин старался обходить болото, а Сталин прёт всегда прямо через болото.

Riddle:
Why did Lenin wear shoes but Stalin boots?

Answer:
Because Lenin preferred to avoid swampy ground and Stalin always opts to slough straight through.[8]

---

[6] For a variant, see HPSSS, no. 32, schedule A, vol. 4, 54.

[7] Allies of N. I. Bukharin (1888–1938), an Old Bolshevik who clashed with Stalin over economic and agricultural policies toward the end of the 1920s.

[8] Variant: "There is an anecdote which says that Lenin always wore shoes and Stalin always wore boots because he walks straight through the mud whereas Lenin always went around the mud puddles." HPSSS, no. 61, schedule A, vol. 5, 50; no. 339, schedule A, vol. 18, 64; no. 379, schedule A, vol. 19, 10; no. 517, schedule A, vol. 26, 24; no. 1493, schedule A, vol. 35, 47; also RGASPI f. 17, op. 120, d. 175, l. 88; f. 17, op. 120, d. 176, l. 137; Gosudarstvennyi arkhiv Novosibirskoi oblasti f. 22, op. 3, d. 520, l. 8ob, cited in Davies, *Public Opinion in Stalin's Russia*, 179.

Figure 13. Lenin and Stalin at the party leader's Gorki sanatorium, 1922

✶ ✶ ✶

На том свете, поблизости от рая, чёрт встречает Сталина и спрашивает:

—Чем опечален, дружок?

—Как же! Вон Маркс в раю, Ленин в раю, а меня не впускают. Помоги, родной

—Сейчас выручу. Полезай в мешок.

Сталин влез в мешок. Чорт взвалил его на плечи и принёс к райским вратам. Спрашивает:

—Ленин тут?

—Тут,—отвечает св. Пётр.

—Вот, возьми его барахло.

In the afterlife, the devil bumps into Stalin standing outside heaven and asks him:

—What's the matter, friend?

—It's so unfair! Marx is in heaven, Lenin's in heaven, and they won't let me in. Please help me!

—Okay. Crawl into this sack.

After Stalin crawls into the sack, the devil slings it over his shoulder and carries it up to the Heavenly Gates. He asks:

—Is Lenin in there?

—Yes—replies St. Peter.

—Here, take this junk of his, will you?

И чорт швырнул мешок в ворота.

And the devil tosses the sack through the gates.[9]

Сталин, глядя на портрет Ленина, спрашивает:
—Ильич, Ильич, что будет с нами?
—Меня снимут, а тебя повесят,— отвечает Ленин.

While looking at a portrait of Lenin, Stalin asks:
—Il'ich, Il'ich, what's to become of us?
Lenin replies:
—They'll pull me down and string you up.

Учитель в школе спрашивает мальчиков, кем хотел бы каждый из них стать, если бы он был сыном Сталина.
Один мальчик пожелал быть героем Советского Союза, другой—маршалом, третий—великим писателем и т.д.
Учитель:
—Ну, а ты?
—Я....Сиротой.

A school teacher asks her boys whom they'd like to become if they were Stalin's sons.
One boy says he'd like to be a Hero of the Soviet Union, while another wants to be a Red Army marshal. A third wants to be a great writer, etc.
The teacher asks still another:
—So, what about you?
—Me? An orphan.[10]

---

[9] Refers to the view that Stalin inherited the party leadership through duplicity. Variants include: "Lenin is knocking on the Gates of Heaven, but they don't let him in. He turns for help to a Jew who was passing by. The Jew puts him in a suitcase and walks up to the Gates of Heaven and knocks. St. Peter comes to the window.
—Is Karl Marx in there?
—Yes.
—Could you ask him to come to the window for a moment?
Karl Marx appears at the window.
—Are you Karl Marx?
—Yes.
—*Capital* is yours?
—Yes.
—Here, take your dividends—and tosses him the suitcase.
"Sovetskie anekdoty," 56; also Karachevtsev, *Dlia nekuriashchikh*, 133; HPSSS, no. 2, schedule A, vol. 1, 38.

[10] Variant: "Once Stalin came incognito to a factory and asked an ordinary worker who his father was. The worker, not knowing it was Stalin asking him, said Stalin is my father. Then Stalin asked, and who is your mother? The worker replied, my mother is the Soviet Union. Then Stalin asked, and what would you like to be? The worker replied, I would like to be an orphan." HPSSS, no. 147, schedule A, vol. 12, 31; also no. 60, schedule A, vol. 5, 33. For a related joke, see I. D. W. Talmadge, "The Enjoyment of Laughter in Russia," *Russian Review* 2: 2 (1943): 50.

☆ ☆ ☆

Один человек вытащил из воды утопавшего, откачал его, а тот и говорит:

—Чем тебя отблагодарить? Проси, чего хочешь. Я—Сталин.

—Боже мой! Какая ошибка вышла. Молю только об одном—никому не говорить, что я Вас спас.

A man drags a drowning person out of the water and resuscitates him. The latter says:

—How can I thank you? I'll do anything you'd like—I'm Stalin.

—Oh God, what have I done? Just one thing, I beg of you: don't tell anyone that I saved you.[11]

☆ ☆ ☆

Сталин однажды неожиданно приказал Поскрёбышеву достать евангелие. Тот достал, приносит. Сталин:

—Найди-ка мне то место, где Христос 10,000 человек накормил 5-ю хлебами. Интересуюсь, как он это сделал....

One day, Stalin unexpectedly orders Poskrebyshev to get him a copy of the Gospels. When Poskrebyshev returns, Stalin says:

—Find the place where Christ feeds 10,000 people with 5 loaves of bread. I'm curious about how he did it....[12]

☆ ☆ ☆

Встречаются два приятеля:
—Ты, кажется, вступил в партию?
Спрошенный, поспешно оглядывая свои ботинки.
—Что ты? Где? Как-будто нет....

Two friends run into each other. One says:

—I heard that you just got into the party.

His friend hurriedly checks the bottoms of his boots.

—Huh? What? Where? No, I don't think I got into anything...[13]

---

[11] Variant: "A Georgian fisherman saves a drowning man who reveals to him that he is Stalin. The fisherman implores him, as a reward, not to let anybody know, or else his compatriots won't accept him." HPSSS, no. 2, schedule A, vol. 1, 38; also no. 25, schedule A, vol. 3, 67; no. 54, schedule A, vol. 5, 28; no. 60, schedule A, vol. 5, 33; no. 62, schedule A, vol. 5, 28; no. 66, schedule A, vol. 6, 67; no. 149, schedule A, vol. 11, 94; no. 639, schedule A, vol. 30, 39.

[12] A. N. Poskrebyshev, Stalin's personal secretary, was apparently to find him the Gospels of Matthew 14:14–21, Mark 6:32–44, Luke 9:10–17, and John 6:1–15.

[13] For a variant attributed to K. B. Radek, see HPSSS, no. 149, schedule A, vol. 11, 94.

FIGURE 14. Red Square Parade

Во время демонстрации на Красной площади в Москве один еврей проходит в колонне мимо трибуны и, повернувшись к «любимым вождям» начинает орать:

—Пламенный привет! Всем пламенный привет!

Его приятель, идущий рядом с ним, шёпотом его одёргивает:

—Хаим, ты сумасшедший! Что ты кричишь и кому?

—Лёва, я нормальный. Не могу же я им кричать прямо: чтоб вы все сгорели!

During a Red Square parade in Moscow, a Jew marching in one of the columns turns toward the "beloved leaders" on the tribune and shouts out:

—Warm greetings! Warm greetings to you all!

His friend, marching next to him, whispers:

—Khaim, are you crazy? What are you yelling? And to whom?

—Lev, I'm fine. It's not like I can say that I wish they'd all burn in hell, is it?[14]

---

[14] Variant: "2 Jews were walking down the street and met an NKVD man. One waved his hand to him and said: '*Plamennyi privet*' [Warm welcome]. When they had passed the NKVD man, the other Jew asked the one who had given this greeting; 'Why did you greet him like that?' And the first answered: '*Ia ne mogu skazat': shtob vy zgoreli!*' [sic, *chtob vy sgoreli*, i.e., I can't say that I wish you'd burn in hell]." HPSSS, no. 9, schedule A, vol. 1, 115.

FIGURE 15. Stalin at the podium

☆ ☆ ☆

В 1929 году, в день своего 50-летия Сталин сказал:

— Я гатов… аддат дэлу рабочего класса… всу сваю кров, каплю зо каплэй.

На это из зала была получена записка: «Тов. Сталин, зачем каплями, отдайте сразу всю».

On the day of his 50th jubilee in 1929, Stalin declares (in heavily accented Russian):

—I am ready to give all my blood for the cause of the working class, drop by drop.

A note is passed up to the podium from the audience that reads: "Com[rade] Stalin, why drop by drop? Why not all at once?"[15]

☆ ☆ ☆

---

[15] For Stalin's actual statement, pledging "all my strength, all my ability, and, if need be, all my blood, drop by drop," see I. Stalin, "Vsem organizatsiiam i tovarishcham, prislavshim privetstviia," *Pravda*, 22 December 1929, p. 1. For variants, see the diary entry from March 11, 1930, in Shitts, *Dnevnik "Velikogo pereloma,"* 175; A. Avtorkhanov, *Stalin and the Soviet Communist Party: A Study in the Technology of Power* (New York: Praeger, 1959), 157.

—Что такое правый уклон?
—Это — лицом к селу.
—А что такое левый уклон?
—Лицом к городу.
—А что такое сталинская «генеральная линия партии»?
—Ни к селу, ни к городу.

—What's the right deviation?
—"Face the village."
—And the left deviation?
—"Face the city."
—What, then, is Stalin's "General Line?"
—Neither here nor there.[16]

В провинциальной партшколе слушатели соревнуются друг с другом в «ортодоксальности»:

—Вы знаете, когда я был в командировке в Москве на прошлой неделе, я видел Карла Маркса на Красной площади в трамвае.

—Ну, это ты, брат, заливаешь: по Красной площади трамваи не ходят.

In a provincial party school, the students competed with one-another to see who was the best communist.

—You know, when I was on a business trip in Moscow last week, I saw Karl Marx in a tram on Red Square.

—Hold on, my friend, who do you think you're kidding? Trams don't run on Red Square.

—Что такое Центральная Контрольная Комиссия?

—Это самое мощное учереждение в СССР.

—Почему?

—Потому, что оно может человека в грязь превратить, а грязь — в человека.

—What is the Central Control Commission?

—It's the most powerful institution in the USSR.

—Why?

—Because it can turn a man into mud and mud into a man.[17]

---

[16] On these policies, see page 47, n. 29.

[17] The Central Control Commission (later known as the Party Control Commission), was an institution responsible for purging party ranks. The last line refers to an idealized version of social mobility under the old regime, when people could supposedly rise from "pauper to prince" (*iz griazi v kniazi*). A variant from the late 1920s asks: "Who's the best chemist in the USSR? Stalin—only he can both create a state official from mud and turn a state official into mud." See the diary entry from March 7, 1928 in Shitts, *Dnevnik "Velikogo pereloma,"* 2; also HPSSS, no. 522, schedule A, vol. 27, 33.

Figure 16. Party purge meeting

Партиец, хорошо известный собранию как *любитель выпить*, проходит чистку:

—Ну, Иванов, как у тебя там с выпивкой дела?

Иванов чистосердечно:

—Да с выпивкой ничего, вот с закуской плохо….

A party member known for being a drinker is being questioned during a purge:

—So, Ivanov, how's it going with the drinking?

Ivanov replies honestly:

—You know, the drinking's okay, but things are getting pretty tough regarding the chaser.

★ ★ ★

Трое служащих проходят чистку. Выясняется, что один из них всегда опаздывает на работу на одну минуту, другой приходит за одну минуту до начала занятий, а третий всегда является точно во-время.

Вычистили всех троих:

Первого—за разгильдяйство,

Второго—за подхалимство,

Третьего—за бюрократизм.

Three office workers are being questioned during a purge. It turns out that one of them is always a minute late to work, another a minute early and the third right on time.

All three are purged from the party:

The first for delinquency,

The second for sycophancy,

The third for bureaucratism.

✯ ✯ ✯

На собрании докладчик распространялся о том, как «мы догоним капиталистические страны». Вопрос из публики:

—А когда догоним, можно там остаться?

A speaker at a meeting goes on and on about how "we're going to catch up to the capitalist countries." Someone asks:

—Once we catch up to them, can we stay there?[18]

✯ ✯ ✯

—Почему в СССР люди разуты?
—Потому, что босому легче догнать и перегнать капиталистические страны.

—Why don't people in the USSR wear shoes?
—Because it's easier to catch up and overtake the capitalist countries running barefoot.[19]

✯ ✯ ✯

Врач в амбулатории выслушивает больного и одновременно заполняет регистрационную карточку.

—Женаты? Дышите…. Член профсоюза? Дышите…. Член партии? Не дышите! Не дышите! …

A doctor examining a patient at a clinic is filling out the fellow's registration card at the same time:

—Are you married? Take a deep breath. Are you a trade union member? Take another deep breath. Are you a party member? Hold your breath. Keep holding it….

✯ ✯ ✯

На многих потребительских кооперативах можно было видеть такие лозунги:

«Кооперация—путь к социализму».
«Социализм—это учёт».

На одном магазине висела также третья вывеска:

«По случаю учёта магазин закрыт».

In many consumer cooperatives, you can see the following slogans:

"Cooperatives are the path to socialism."

"Socialism is accounting."

But in one store, there was also a third sign:

"Co-op closed for accounting."[20]

---

[18] For a variant, see Azov, "Satira pod spudom," 2.

[19] Variant: "In Moscow at the time of the 16th Party Congress Stalin was asked many questions and there were two he could not answer. 1) Why is there so little cattle and meat in the USSR and 2) Why aren't there enough shoes? When he could not answer the questions, he went to the Kremlin to think and met a Jew who asked him what the trouble was. After hearing the questions [the Jew] told Stalin to answer: 1) We have no cattle because it is all gathered in Moscow for the 16th Party Congress and 2) if we must overtake and surpass the Americans, it is easier to run without shoes." HPSSS, no. 54, schedule A, vol. 5, 28.

Покупатель, выходя из вновь открытого универмага:

—И чего, чего только у нас нет: масла нет, сахара нет, мяса нет, одежды нет, обуви нэт....

A customer, exiting a newly-opened supermarket, exclaims:

—Is there nothing that we don't have for sale? We don't have butter, we don't have sugar, we don't have meat, we don't have clothes, we don't have shoes....[21]

☆ ☆ ☆

В Ленинграде театр «Комедия» помещался над Елисеевским магазином, в котором всегда было либо пусто, либо втридорога.

Говорили так:

«Наверху—комедия, а внизу—трагедия.»

In Leningrad, the Comedy Theater was located above the Eliseevskii Store, which was always either empty or three times more expensive than other stores. People often said:

—It's comedy above and tragedy below.

---

[20] For a variant, see the diary entry from February 18, 1929, in Shitts, *Dnevnik "Velikogo pereloma,"* 90; HPSSS, no. 66, schedule B, vol. 23, 35.

[21] For variants, see HPSSS, no. 1498, schedule A, vol. 35, 17; *Sovetskie anekdoty*, 18.

Collectivization

A key component of Stalin's "revolution from above" was the establishment of central state control over agriculture. Official attempts to shift the terms of trade to the state's advantage during the second half of the 1920s had driven the peasantry to withdraw their grain from the market, precipitating shortages and bread rationing in urban centers by the end of the decade. Determined to nip this peasant resistance in the bud, the party declared war on its perceived enemies in the countryside, the *kulaks* (usually influential village leaders and the rural clergy) and announced plans for the collectivization of peasant agriculture around the model of the collective farm.

Transforming the peasantry from independent agriculturalists into rural employees of the state assured the party leadership a monopoly over grain supplies, but at great cost to both agricultural productivity and peasant society as a whole. Collectivization and dekulakization, compounded by the 1932–33 famine that these policies triggered, ultimately claimed several million lives and left the countryside broken and impoverished. Such circumstances explain the sense of profound fatalism that dominate collectivization-oriented humor from the early 1930s.

Двое встречаются в 1930 году и спрашивают друг друга по обыкновению:
—Как Вы живёте?
Те же встречаются в 1931 году:
—*Как* Вы живёте?
Те же встречаются в 1932 году:
—Как?! Вы живёте?!

Two people meet in 1930 and exchange niceties:
—How're you getting by?
They meet in 1931:
—*How* are you getting by?
They meet in 1932:
—You're getting by? How?[1]

★ ★ ★

---

[1] Variant: "One muscovite meets another and asks 'How are you doing (*kak zhivesh'*)?' 'Like Lenin.' 'What do you mean "Like Lenin?"' 'That is simple: they have not buried me, but they are [also] not giving me anything to eat.'" HPSSS, no. 305, schedule A, vol. 15, 74.

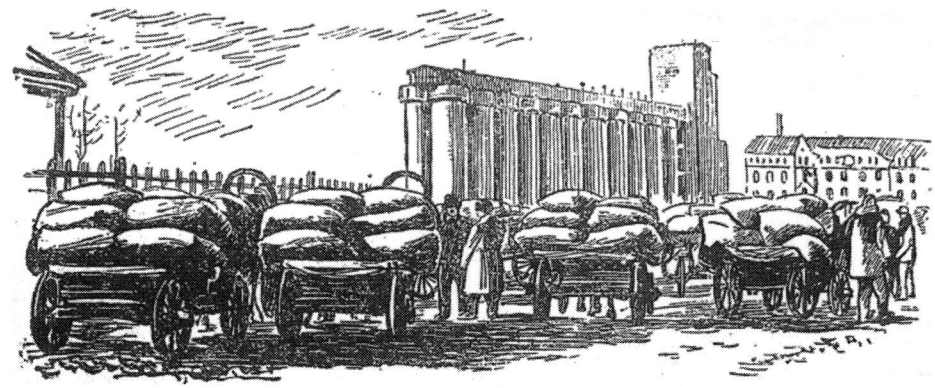

Figure 17. Collective farm grain being delivered to the state

Старый колхозник объясняет:

—Вот наша колхозная жизнь!

Подбрасывает пригоршню зерна и ловит ладонью

—Вот что остаётся после госпоставок!

Подбрасывает то, что осталось на ладони, и ловит тыльной частью руки:

—А вот, что остаётся после выделения семфондов.

Подбрасывает зерно снова и ловит несколько зёрнышек ребром руки:

—А вот, что остаётся на трудодни....

A veteran collective farmer explains:

—This is how we live on a collective farm.

He throws a handful of grain into the air and catches some in the palm of his hand.

—This is how much is left after the state takes its share.

He then throws what is in his palm up into the air and catches what he can on the back of his hand.

—That is what's left after putting grain away for the spring planting.

He then throws that grain up into the air and catches what he can on the side of his hand.

—And this is what we get for our work....

Крестьянин спрашивает в лавке гвоздей:

—Никаких гвоздей нет.

—Вот то же и наш предколхоза говорил: «вперёд к коммунизму, и никаких гвоздей».

A peasant goes into a store in search of cigarettes:

—We don't have anything… not even cigarette butts.

—Ah, now I understand why our collective farm chairman says "Forward to communism and no ifs, ands, or buts."

Колхозник подходит к часовому у кремлёвской стены и спрашивает:

—Скажи, сынок, для чего такая высокая стена?

Часовой сердито:

—А чтоб через неё разбойники не лазили.

—Отсюда туда или оттуда сюда?

A collective farmer goes up to a guard at the Kremlin Gate and asks:

—Tell me, sonny, what's this high wall for?

The guard responds angrily:

—So that bandits won't get over it.

—Coming or going?[2]

Приехавший в Москву колхозник спрашивает у милиционера:

—Что это за стена, и почему перед ней стоят солдаты?

—Это Кремль. Не показывай пальцем!

—А кто же там?

—Сталин.

—А... зачем солдаты?

—Это охрана.

—А-а... понимаю, понимаю... Ну, теперь-то он, сволочь, оттуда не выскочит!

A collective farmer who's just arrived in Moscow asks a police officer:

—What's that wall for and why are there soldiers standing in front of it?"

—That's the Kremlin. Don't point so obviously!

—Who's in there?

—Stalin.

—What's with all the soldiers?

—They're standing guard.

—Ah, I see. Well, now that bastard won't be able to escape any more.[3]

* * *

---

[2] Variant: "A father and his little boy were walking one day outside the walls of the Kremlin. The little boy turned to his father and asked him: Father, why are the walls of the Kremlin so high? The father replied to the son: Sonny, the walls of the Kremlin are so high so that the bandits can't get over them. And the little boy, he could not have been more than five years old, looked up at his father and said: You mean so the bandits can't get from inside the Kremlin to the outside, Daddy?" HPSSS, no. 8, schedule A, vol. 1, 35–36; also no. 80, schedule A, vol. 6, 12; no. 80, schedule B, vol. 14, 12.

[3] Variant: "Three lines of foreign troops are surrounding the home of Stalin's mother in Gori near Tiflis. And someone asked why these three lines of foreign troops were surrounding the home and the person [said that he] thought that the troops were there in order to protect Stalin's mother from possible harm. However, another person answered—no. They're here to see that she doesn't give birth to another like him." HPSSS, no. 11, schedule A, vol. 2, 50; also no. 66, schedule A, vol. 6, 67–68; no. 639, schedule A, vol. 30, 39.

FIGURE 18. Kalinin and a group of collective farmers

Крестьяне пришли к Калинину жаловаться на то, что нигде ничего нельзя купить. Говорят:

—Вот заграницей всего можно достать....

—Э, послушайте, это известная история: хорошо там, где нас нет.

—И мы тоже так думаем, Михаил Иванович, хорошо там, где вас нет.

Some peasants go to Kalinin[4] to complain that there isn't anything in the stores. They say:

—In other countries, people can get anything they want....

—You know, this sounds like the old adage that the grass is always greener when you're on the other side of the fence.

—You're exactly right, Mikhail Ivanovich. When *you're* on the other side of the fence, the grass *is* always greener.[5]

При другом визите колхозников к Калинину они жаловались так:

—Товарищ Калинин, жить невозможно, ходим ободраны, босы....

Калинин успокаивает:

—Ничего, товарищи, потерпите.

During another audience with Kalinin, some peasants complained:

—Comrade Kalinin, it's impossible to live like this. We walk around in rags and barefoot.

Kalinin tries to console them:

---

[4] See page 51 n. 1.

[5] For related jokes, see Karachevtsev, *Dlia nekuriashchikh*, 152; Talmadge, "The Enjoyment of Laughter in Russia," 50.

FIGURE 19. Audience with Kalinin

Ещё не так плохо. Есть страны, где люди ходят совсем голыми....

—А там, Михаил Иванович, советская власть, наверно, лет уж 50 как существует?!

—That's nothing, comrades, be patient. It's not that bad. The are some countries where people walk around entirely naked.

—How long have the Soviets been in power there, Mikhail Ivanovich? Fifty years?[6]

Эстрадник поёт: «Укажи мне такую обитель, где бы русский мужик не страдал». Колхозник в зале:

An entertainer sings: "Show me a single place where the Russian peasant has not suffered."

---

[6] Variant: "A peasant who came from the same district as Kalinin and who knew Kalinin before he became the chairman of the Soviet visited him in the Kremlin and [...] said, 'Look, we have no clothing, we are going around half naked. Can't you get us some clothing? Get us some material for the villagers.' Kalinin said 'Well, I can't help you, because I have nothing now. Perhaps in the future I will be able to help you.' And then to ease the peasant['s mind,] he said 'Look, in India they go completely naked and they don't think anything of it.' At this the peasant turned to him and asked him 'Well, and how long have they had the Soviet power?'" HPSSS, no. 1, schedule A, vol. 1, 26–27; also no. 3, schedule A, vol. 1, 29; no. 5, schedule A, vol. 1, 17; no. 8, schedule A, vol. 1, 23; no. 25, schedule A, vol. 1, 17; no. 25, schedule A, vol. 3, 68; no. 66, schedule A, vol. 6, 67; no. 1240, schedule A, vol. 32, 44; no. 1486, schedule A, vol. 34, 39; Lyons, *Moscow Carousel*, 331–32.

—Калинин в Кремле.

A collective farmer from the audience grumbles:

—Kalinin in the Kremlin.[7]

На приёме у Калинина делегация колхозников спросила его, что значит слово «темпы». Калинин объяснил:

—Вот посмотрите в окно, видите, выезжает из ворот один автомобиль. Через год из тех же ворот выедут 10 машин, через 2 года—100 машин и так далее.

Делегация вернулась в колхоз и начала агитировать «за темпы». На общем собрании колхозники спрашивают, что такое «темпы». Один из делегатов объясняет:

—Вот, посмотрите в окно, видите... стоит крест на могиле. Через год будет 10 крестов, через 2 года—100 и так далее....

During an audience with Kalinin, a delegation of collective farm workers asks what the term "tempos" means. Kalinin explains:

—Take a look out the window. See that car driving through the gate? In a year, ten cars will be driving through that gate and in 2 years, 100 cars, and so on.

After the delegation returns to their collective farm, they begin to promote the concept of "increasing tempos" at a general assembly. The collective farmers ask what "tempos" are. One of the delegates replies:

—Take a look out the window.... See the cross over that grave? In a year, there will be 10 crosses, in two years, there'll be 100, and so on.[8]

Колхозник вернулся из Москвы домой и с воодушевлением рассказывает:

—Чудеса, братки! Раньше за 3 года

A collective farmer returns home from Moscow and announces with amazement:

—It's a miracle, my brothers! They're

---

[7] For variants, see the diary entry from May 12, 1928 in Shitts, *Dnevnik "Velikogo pereloma,"* 23; HPSSS, no. 62, schedule A, vol. 5, 28–30.

[8] Variant: "A kolkhoznik was sent to Moscow to take a course in which the 5–year plan would be explained to him. When he [got] to the institute they explained his political questions and talked and talked to him. But the kolkhoznik could not understand [anything]. The teacher said to him: 'I see that it is difficult to explain [this] to you, so I will give you a concrete example. Suppose you went on the street and you saw a car go by. This is the 5-year plan. In the first 5-year plan you would see one car. But in the second five-year plan there would be two of them.' So the peasant went back to the kolkhoz having finished the course. When he got there the other kolkhozniks asked him what the 5-year plan was about and he told them: 'I will give you an example. Suppose you go out in the fields and there you see the body of a dead cow. In the first five years there would be only one dead cow, but in the second there would be two.'" HPSSS, no. 48, schedule A, vol. 5, 63; also no. 52, schedule A, vol. 5, 29–30; no. 1011, schedule A, vol. 31, 17.

такого дома не выстроили бы, какой теперь за 3 месяца строят.

Сосед перебивает его:

—Это ничего. У нас чудеса почище— погляди на наше кладбище. Раньше его за 50 лет не заполнили бы, а теперь за 3 года полно.

building now in 3 months what would have taken three years to build before.

A neighbor interrupts him:

—That's nothing. We've got even more wondrous miracles here. Take a look at our graveyard. Before, it'd have taken us 50 years to fill it as full as we have during the past 3.[9]

В захолустный колхоз приехал докладчик из района. Колхозников согнали в «клуб»; колхозное начальство уселось в «президиум»; докладчик развернул свои шпаргалки и начал. Он не проговорил и пяти минут, как председатель колхоза внезапно поднялся и заорал:

—Встать!

Двигая стульями, колхозники все поднялись. Председатель обвёл всех строгим взглядом:

—Сесть.

Колхозники сели. Докладчик недоумённо посмотрел на председателя, потом в шпаргалки и продолжал. Через пять минут председатель опять:

—Встать!!

Колхозники, расталкивая друг друга, снова поднялись.

—Сесть!!

Через каждые пять минут председатель орал: «встать» и «сесть». Докладчик кое-как «закруглился» и подходит к председателю:

—Почему ты меня прерывал своими «встать», «сесть»?

A speaker arrives at a distant collective farm and the collective farmers are herded into the "club" while the leadership assembles into a "presidium" on stage. The speaker unfolds his crib notes and begins. He's spoken for less than five minutes, however, when the collective farm chairman suddenly stands up and shouts:

—Atten-tion!

Pushing back their chairs, the collective farmers all stand up at attention. The chairman sweeps across the room with a stern gaze.

—Be seated.

The collective farmers sit down. The speaker looks incredulously at the chairman and then at his notes and continues. Five minutes later, the chairman again yells out:

—Atten-tion!!

The collective farmers, bumping into one-another, again stand up.

—Be seated!!

Every five minutes the chairman continues to cry out "Attention" and "Be seated." The speaker somehow finishes and then goes up to the chairman.

---

[9] Variant: "One collective farmer is explaining to another collective farmer why everything has to be done in 4 years, and pointed to the sanatorium [sic, asylum] and said 'That has to be filled in 4 years instead of 5.'" HPSSS, no. 19, schedule A, vol. 2, 20. In the fall of 1929, party officials started calling for the first Five-Year Plan to be fulfilled in four years.

FIGURE 20. Collective farm assembly

—Да спят, сволочи, не видишь, что-ли?

—Why were you continuously interrupting me with your "Attention" and "Be seated?"

— Didn't you notice? The bastards were all sound asleep!

В деревню приехал партагитататор. Колхозников согнали в «клуб» слушать «лекцию». Она длилась три часа, в течение которых агитатор выпил 5 стаканов воды. Наконец, «лекция» кончилась, и колхозники облегчённо двинулись к двери. Но… встал председатель колхоза.

—Есть ли вопросы по существу?
Все молчат. Председатель:

—Активность мала, товарищи колхозники. Подождём, пока не станут задавать вопросы по существу.

A party agitator arrives in a village. The collective farmers are herded into the "club," where they're to listen to a "lecture." This lecture lasts three hours, during which the agitator drinks five glasses of water. Finally, the "lecture" draws to a close and the collective farmers begin moving toward the door with relief. But then the collective farm chairman rises to his feet.

—Questions, anyone?
All are silent. The chairman says:
—You should be more engaged,

Напряжённое молчание. Наконец, в заднем ряду кто-то не вытерпел:

—У меня есть вопрос по-существу: товарищ начальник, вот Вы говорили, выпили 5 стаканов воды. Не хочется ли Вам сходить куда-нибудь?

Председатель строго:

—Не трепитесь, задавайте серьёзные вопросы.

Другой голос:

—А в котором часу в городе пивные закрываются?

comrade collective farmers. Nobody will leave until we get some serious questions.

There's a tense silence. Finally, someone in the back row can't resist any longer:

—I have a question. Comrade Boss, while you were talking, you drank five glasses of water. Don't you need to excuse yourself?

The chairman says sternly:

—Stop fooling around and ask a serious question.

A second voice:

—What time do the taverns in town close tonight?[10]

На собрании предколхоза объявляет о награждении лучших ударников. Одну доярку наградили радиоприёмником, другой дали граммофон, третьей— велосипед.

Все аплодируют, доярки счастливы. Председатель колхоза поднимается и особо торжественно объявляет:

—А теперь, товарищи, наградим нашу самую лучшую ударницу, которая есть политически сознательная, работала без праздников и выходных, поставила рекорд по выкормке поросят; она есть пример для всех остальных. Наградим нашу свинарку Дарью (тут голос председателя задрожал)… сборником сочинений тов. Сталина!

Собрание замерло.

Голос сзади:

—Так ей, стерве, и надо.

A collective farm chairman was presenting awards to his best shock workers at an assembly. One milkmaid is awarded a radio, a second is given a record player and a third gets a bicycle. Everyone applauds and the milkmaids are pleased.

The chairman then rises to his feet and announces in an especially grand way:

—And now, comrades, we recognize our very best shock worker, who is politically conscious, who's worked without holidays and other days off, and who's set a record for feeding piglets— she's an example for us all. I hereby award our swineherd Daria (here the chairman's voice trembles)… a collection of Comrade Stalin's speeches!

The meeting goes silent.

In the back, someone mutters:

—Just what the bitch deserves.[11]

---

[10] For a related joke, see HPSSS, no. 108, schedule B, vol. 15, 21.

[11] See also HPSSS, no. 65, schedule B, vol. 3, 30.

FIGURE 21. Collective farmers listening to a portable radio

Ещё не закончилась коллективизация в районе, как в одном колхозе началась установка радиоузла. Крестьянин робко подходит к технику и спрашивает:

—Товарищ, а «оно» передаёт без проводов?

—Без проводов.

—И везде будет слышно?

—Везде.

—И заграницей?

—И заграницей.

Крестьянин быстро подбегает к микрофону:

—Спасите, грабят!!!

A collective farm began to set up a radio station even before the district was completely collectivized. A peasant timidly comes up to the technician and asks:

—Comrade, does this thing transmit without cables?

—Yes, without cables.

—And will it be audible everywhere?

—Yes, everywhere.

—Even abroad?

—Yes, even abroad.

Dashing to the microphone, the peasant yells:

—Stop, thief!

Плакат в «Доме Крестьянина»:
«Спи скорей, твоя подушка нужна другому.»

A poster in a peasants' dormitory:
"Sleep faster—someone else is waiting for your pillow."[12]

☆ ☆ ☆

На советско-польской границе блоха встречает свинью. Свинья спрашивает:
—Ты откуда бежишь?
—Бегу из Германии. Немцы всё чистят, моют, просто житья нет. А ты?
—А я бегу из СССР. Чуть не подохла с голоду—весь мой корм люди сожрали.

On the Soviet-Polish border, a flea runs into a pig. The pig asks:
—Where are you running from?
—From Germany. The Germans are cleaning and scrubbing everything. There's nowhere left to live. And you?
—Well, I'm escaping from the USSR. I just about starved to death when people started to eat up all my slop.

☆ ☆ ☆

Трудно поверить газетам, что один советский колхозник дожил до 140 лет. От советской власти годы жизни не прибавляются, а только кажутся длиннее.

It's difficult to believe the papers when they say that a Soviet collective farmer has lived to be 140 years old. Soviet power doesn't actually add years to one's life—it just makes them seem longer.

---

[12] Originally a Yiddish proverb, this one-liner forms the core of Zoshchenko's short story "Spi skorei" (1935–37).

Industrialization

Collectivization in the countryside was matched by a redoubled effort to expand the USSR's industrial sector during the late 1920s and early 1930s. Recruitment of a new generation of factory hands was intended to swell the ranks of the working class and replace the last vestiges of the traditional, peasant economy with a rational, forward-looking vision of the proletarian future. Party propagandists routinely conflated the idea of socialist construction with industrialization, making it difficult to envision one without the other. Ambitious Five-Year Plan targets predicted economic productivity to double, accompanied by a 65 percent increase in wage levels. Although many must have looked upon such claims with skepticism, few realized the extent to which such wildly unrealistic expectations diverged from reality. A massive influx of new workers into the economy and enormous labor turnover obscured the fact that urban standards of living plummeted by as much as 50 percent during these years.

Many reconciled themselves to such hardships, viewing them as a temporary phenomenon linked to the construction of socialism and a wave of sabotage and "wrecking" perpetrated by embittered class enemies. Still, this didn't stop political humorists of the era from lampooning the hyperbole surrounding the Stakhanovite hero-workers and "accomplishments" of the Five-Year Plan. They also waxed ironic about the "proletarian dictatorship's" exploitation of the Soviet working class, whether in terms of labor discipline, wage inequalities, or the coercive nature of "voluntary" state bond drives. That said, even as jokesters were laying bare the dysfunctional aspects of the Five-Year Plan, they only rarely challenged the fundamental goal of state-led industrialization or called for a return to an agrarian way of life.

В СССР 8-часовой рабочий день: с 8 утра до 8 вечера.

In the USSR, the 8-hour working day stretches from 8 a.m. to 8 p.m.

✸ ✸ ✸

Figure 22. Workers' assembly

Коммунист-начальник оставляет голодного рабочего на сверхсрочную работу.

—Устал я, тов. начальник, отдохнуть бы….

—Отдохнём на том свете.

A communist boss refuses to relieve a hungry worker engaged in an urgent task.

—But I'm exhausted, comrade. I need a break.

—We'll rest when we get to heaven.

В одном учреждении начальник обходит служащих и спрашивает одного строго:

—Тов. Николаев, почему Вы сегодня опоздали на службу?

—Я… извините, заспался.

—Это не причина—выспаться Вы могли бы и на службе.

The director of a state institution comes up to one of his office workers and asks him sternly:

—Comrade Nikolaev, why were you late today?

—I'm sorry, I overslept.

—That's no excuse. You can catch up on your sleep at work.

☆ ☆ ☆

На собрании докладчик расписывает яркими красками все блага, которые принесёт трудящимся пятилетка. Он даже упоминает про целых «два килограмма мяса на человека».

Слушатели, как всегда, сидят молча, неподвижно, тупо уставившись в землю. Наконец, из задних рядов кто-то спрашивает:

—Товарищ докладчик, извините я не расслышал. Вы сказали, что через 5 лет будет по два килограмма мяса на человека или на человеке?

At a meeting, a speaker was outlining in bright colors all the benefits that the Five-Year Plan was going to extend to workers. He even reminded them of the slogan "two kilos of meat per person." The audience, as always, sat silent and motionless, staring blankly at the floor. Finally, from the last row, someone asked:

—Comrade speaker, excuse me, but I couldn't quite hear. Did you say that in five years each person is going to get two kilos or that each person's going to weigh two kilos?

☆ ☆ ☆

Как в Торгсине на витрине
Есть и сыр, и колбаса,
А в рабочем магазине
«Солнце, воздух и вода».
Или:
Как в Торгсине на витрине
Есть и сыр, и колбаса,
…А рабочий от досады
Рвёт на ж… волоса.

Although Torgsin's[1] got
Both sausage and cheese,
The workers' stores have naught
But "sun, water and a breeze."
    Or:
Although Torgsin's got
Both sausage and cheese,
The workers will get naught
But dick for their pleas.

☆ ☆ ☆

В царское время люди 6 дней работали, один день отдыхали.

При советской власти начали 5 дней работать, один отдыхать («шестидневка»).

Сейчас 4 дня работаем, один отдыхаем («пятидневка»).

Надеемся, что по мере движения к светлому будущему—коммунизму—

In tsarist times, people worked for 6 days and had one day off.

Under Soviet power, people began by working for 5 days and had one day off (the six-day week).

Now, we work 4 days on and have one day off (the five-day week).[2]

We hope that as we advance toward the bright future and communism,

---

[1] A network of stores that allowed Soviet citizens and foreigners to buy hard-to-find goods and food in trade for foreign currency, valuables, and family heirlooms. Proceeds were sold abroad to finance industrialization.

[2] In August 1929, the party introduced the 5-day week, ostensibly to undermine observation of the Christian Sabbath. Some felt it was also a way of reducing the number of

FIGURE 23. Shop floor production meeting

будем:
3 дня работать, один отдыхать,
2 дня работать, один отдыхать,
1 день работать, один отдыхать;
а при коммунизме будем…
12 часов работать и 12 отдыхать.

we will:
Work for 3 days and have one day off,
Work for 2 days and have one day off,
Work 1 day and have one day off;
And then under communism, we'll…
work for 12 hours and then have 12
hours off.

[В июне 1931 года Сталин
провозгласил свои «шесть условий»
построения социалистической
промышленности: правильно набрать
рабочую силу; эффективно
организовать зарплату; улучшить
организацию труда; воспитать новую

[In June 1931, Stalin announced "six
conditions" needed for socialist
industrialization: adequate manpower,
reconfigured wages, effective
organization, efficient accounting, the
cooperation of the old technical
intelligentsia, and the training of a new

days off that workers enjoyed during the week—see the diary entry from September
25, 1929, in Shitts, *Dnevnik "Velikogo pereloma,"* 143.

интеллигенцию из рабочего класса; улучшить отношение к старой интеллигенции; урепить хозрасчет.] К «шести условиям» народ придумал пять добавочных:

7. Солнечное отопление
8. Лунное освещение
9. Заочное питание
10. Райское одеяние и
11. Гробовое молчание.

technical intelligentsia.[3]] The people thought up five additional conditions:

7. sufficient sunlight for warmth
8. enough moonlight for illumination
9. the ability to eat in absentia
10. the existence of heavenly rainments
11. the wisdom to be silent like the grave.[4]

☆ ☆ ☆

Были предложены также «шесть заповедей» для безопасности советского гражданина:

1. Не думай
2. Если подумал, не говори
3. Если сказал, не записывай
4. Если написал, не печатай
5. Если напечатал, не подписывай
6. Если подписал, отрекись.

There were also "six commandments" proposed for Soviet citizens' safety.

1. Don't think.
2. If you've had a thought, don't say it out loud.
3. If you've said it out loud, don't write it down.
4. If you've written it down, don't publish it.
5. If you've published it, don't sign it.
6. If you've signed it, renounce it.

☆ ☆ ☆

В здании Госплана случился пожар. Начальник орёт благим матом:
—Спасайте потоло-о-к!

A fire breaks out at Gosplan. The director yells at the top of his lungs:
—Save as much air as you can![5]

☆ ☆ ☆

—Иван Иванович, что это у Вас в кабинете липой пахнет?
—Пятилетний план составляю.

—Ivan Ivanovich, what's in your office that smells so rotten?
—I'm putting together a Five-Year Plan.

☆ ☆ ☆

---

[3] I. Stalin, "Novaia obstanovka—novye zadachi khoziaistvennogo stroitel'stva (Rech' na soveshchanii khoziaistvennikov 23 iiunia 1931 goda)," *Pravda*, 5 July 1931, p. 1.

[4] For references to this joke, see the diary entry from December 30, 1929, in Shitts, *Dnevnik "Velikogo pereloma,"* 162; the diary entry from July 24, 1933 in Man'kov, "Iz dnevnika riadovogo cheloveka," 151; HPSSS, no. 446, schedule B, vol. 13, 34.

[5] According to popular belief, Gosplan, the State Planning Agency, made up its figures out of thin air (lit.: "off the ceiling").

Говорят, в «Вечерней Москве» было помещено следующее объявление:
«Временно требуется инженер—строитель социализма. Обращаться по адресу: Москва, Кремль, Сталинский тупик».

It's said that the following advertisement appeared in *Evening Moscow*:
"Wanted: an engineer to build socialism. Applications accepted at the following address: Stalin's Dead-End, the Kremlin, Moscow."

☆ ☆ ☆

В начале НЭПа Ленин говорил: либо капитализм пересилит социализм, либо наоборот: кто—кого?
Во время 2-ой пятилетки «счастливые советские граждане» говорили:
Первая пятилетка—кто кого; вторая пятилетка—кого куда.

At the beginning of NEP, Lenin said that either capitalism would win out over socialism or socialism would win out over capitalism. The question was, who'll beat whom?
During the second Five-Year Plan, the "happy Soviet citizens" said to one-another:
—During the first Five-Year Plan, it was who'll beat whom; under the second Five-Year Plan, it's now who'll be sent where.

☆ ☆ ☆

—Вы стоите за пятилетку?
—А что же вы хотите, чтобы я за нее сидел?

—Do you stand in support of the Five-Year Plan?
—What would you prefer? That I sat in prison because of it?

☆ ☆ ☆

Утёсов (известный в СССР юморист) с эстрады рассказывает:
—Живем мы, слава Богу, не худо. Я треплюсь вот так каждый вечер—тысяч 10 в месяц зарабатываю. Доченька моя, безголосая Эдитка, иногда пищит в джазе—тысячи две зарабатывает. Так что, в общем, неплохо живем…. Да вот, еще, чуть не забыл, муж её, инженер, человек

Utesov,[6] a famous Soviet comedian, told the following story from the stage:
—Thank God, my family doesn't live all that badly. I ramble on like this every night and get something like 10 thousand rubles a month. My daughter, Editka, who's got no voice, sometimes squeaks out a bit of jazz, and makes about two thousand…. Oh yes, I almost forgot… there's also her husband, an engineer, a "highly

---

[6] L. O. Utesov (1895–1982), a jazz musician and performer.

FIGURE 24. Tractor drivers' political literacy circle, Turkmenistan

очень серьёзный, «высококвалифициро-
ванный специалист», часов по 12 в день
работает, тот тоже рублей 600 в месяц
получает....

qualified specialist," who works 12
hours a day. He also makes about 600
a month....[7]

☆ ☆ ☆

Парторганизатор на собрании
уверяет, что ещё через какую-нибудь
пару лет пятилеток у многих советских
граждан не только автомобили, но даже
собственные самолёты будут.
Увлечённый этой картиной
процветания слушатель:
— Вот житуха-то будет: скажу,
Манька, заводи ероплан, слыхать в

A party organizer predicts at a
meeting that after a couple of years of
the Five-Year Plan, many Soviet citizens
will not only have their own cars, but
their own airplanes as well. One listener
gets carried away with this picture of
prosperity:
— Wow, that'll be the life. I'll say,
Man'ka, go get the airplane warmed up.

---

[7] For related jokes, see HPSSS, no. 3, schedule A, vol. 1, 30; no. 610, schedule B, vol. 20,
3.

[8] For variants, see the diary entry from May 13, 1929, in Shitts, *Dnevnik "Velikogo pereloma,"* 115; Karachevtsev, *Dlia nekuriashchikh,* 139.

Харькоге по 9-му талону кислую капусту дают....

I hear that in Khar'kov, you can use ration ticket #9 to get sauerkraut....[8]

На митинге оратор:

—Товарищи, под водительством нашего мудрого вождя великого Сталина, мы строим сейчас гидростанцию в Кобылятах!

Голос с места:

—А как же там гидростанцию, когда там реки нет?

Оратор строго:

—Ну, товарищ, Вы газет не читаете.

—Да это газеты, я родом оттуда....

—Антисоветскую агитацию бросим, гражданин!

A speaker announces at a rally:

—Comrades, under the direction of our wise leader, the great Stalin, we are now building a hydroelectric power plant in Kobyliaty![9]

Someone in the crowd calls out:

—How can you put a hydroelectric power station there if there's no river?

The speaker replies sternly:

—Comrade, haven't you been reading the papers?

—Why should I read the papers? I was born there.

—Drop your anti-Soviet agitation, citizen![10]

Иностранцу показывают советскую фабрику—объясняют, что она работает в три смены, что там есть ударничество, соцсоревнование, высокая производительность, всё это «под мудрым руководством» и пр. и пр. Иностранец спрашивает:

—А что же фабрика выпускает?

—Эмалированные дощечки.

A foreigner visiting a Soviet factory is told that its workers work all three shifts, that they engage in shock work and socialist competition, that they have a high level of productivity, and that this all takes place "under wise leadership," etc., etc. The foreigner asks:

—And what does the factory produce?

—Enamel signs.

---

[9] Perhaps Andreevich meant Kobeliaki, a Ukrainian city near Poltava.

[10] Variant: Kalinin "is making a speech in Moscow about the great industrial advance of the country. With especial fervor he describes the brand-new twenty-storey [sic] skyscrapers on Karl Marx Street in Kharkhov. 'Comrade Kalinin,' a worker in the audience protests meekly, 'I live in Kharkov. Every day, almost, I take a long walk on Karl Marx Street and I have not seen any such skyscrapers.' 'That's the trouble with you,' Kalinin replies indignantly. 'You waste your time promenading instead of reading the newspapers and learning what is going on in the country.'" Lyons, *Moscow Carousel*, 332. For another variant, see HPSSS, no. 11, schedule A, vol. 2, 31.

В цехе действительно лежала гора дощечек. Вот таких: «лифт не работает».

And sure enough, there was a mountain of little signs on the shop floor which read: "Elevator out of service."[11]

Первый крематорий, построенный в Москве, торжественно вводили в эксплуатацию. Калинин объяснял иностранцам:

—Крематорий целиком построен руками советских инженеров и из советских материалов. Сейчас вы увидите, как он действует. Трупчика, извиняюсь, подходящего сегодня нет. Нашли вот замёрзшего беспризорника.

Беспризорника кладут в гроб, гроб вдвигают в печь, включают огонь и выдерживают 5 минут.

Калинин с сияющим лицом:

—Сейчас вы увидите результат кремации.

Открывают печь... гроб цел. Приоткрывают гроб. Оттуда голос беспризорника:

—Закрой крышку, зараза, а то дует!

Moscow's first crematorium opened for business amid great fanfare. At the ceremony, Kalinin takes the foreign guests aside and explains:

—This crematorium has been constructed entirely by Soviet engineers using Soviet materials. You'll now have a chance to see how it works. I apologize for the fact that we don't have a suitable corpse today. But we do have the body of a homeless orphan who's frozen to death.

They put the orphan in a coffin, roll it into the furnace, ignite the burners and wait 5 minutes. Kalinin then says with a radiant face:

—Now you will see the results of the cremation.

They open the furnace... and the coffin emerges unscathed. They lift the lid to peek into the coffin and hear a voice from inside:

—Close the lid, you bastards. There's a draft!

По приказанию Сталина в Кремле были оборудованы новейшего типа «гигиенические» уборные. В них дверь можно было открыть изнутри только после спуска воды.

Однажды перед заседанием Политбюро Сталин вышел в уборную. Собравшиеся ждали 5 минут, 10 минут, 20 минут—Сталин не появляется.

Пошли кликать его. Сталин отзывается из уборной:

On Stalin's order, the Kremlin was equipped with a new type of "hygienic" bathroom. Once occupied, it would lock and remain locked until after the toilet had been flushed. Once, just before a Politburo meeting, Stalin went to the bathroom. Those assembled waited 5 minutes, 10 minutes, 20 minutes, and Stalin still didn't appear. They went to knock on the door and heard Stalin's voice from inside:

---

[11] For a variant, see Sokolova, "Strana moego detstva," 357.

—Не могу выйти, воды нет.

—I'm trapped. The plumbing's acted up and there's no water.[12]

О качестве советской продукции:
Спички шведские,
Головки советские.
Пять минут вонь,
А потом огонь.

On the quality of Soviet goods:
The match sticks are French,
But the Soviet heads are a fright.
Five minutes of stench,
And then finally a light.

Цыгану предлагают подписаться на заём. Он отказывается. Его увещевают:
—Помоги советской власти.
—Какая же это власть, если она даже у цыган денег просит?!

A gypsy is asked to sign up for a state bond. He refuses. They try to convince him:
—Come on, help out Soviet power!
—What sort of a power can it be if it's begging for money even from gypsies?

* * *

Два советских гражданина обсуждают какое-то новое мероприятие «любимого правительства».
—А как ты думаешь, это будет добровольно?
—Да... как на заём.

Two Soviet citizens are discussing a new campaign sponsored by their "beloved government."
—What do you think? Will it be voluntary?
—Yes... just like the bond issues.[13]

* * *

Из газетной хроники:
«Найден труп. Никаких следов насилия, кроме двух облигаций госзайма, на нём не обнаружено».

From a newspaper article:
"A corpse has been found. No signs of violence were uncovered except for two state bonds."[14]

* * *

---

[12] This is based on a short story by M. M. Zoshchenko, "Zapadnia" (1933).

[13] Soviets referred to state bonds as "voluntary-but-compulsory" (*dobrovol'no v obiazatel'nom poriadke*). One former Soviet citizen explained that this stemmed from an incident in which an official in charge of a bond subscription had apparently told some workers that they should "sign up voluntarily, according to their conscience," hinting that they should be conscious of what would happen if they didn't. See HPSSS no. 5, schedule A, vol. 1, 24.

[14] Variant: "The corpse of a drowned man was discovered in the Moscow River. No signs of force were found on the body except for two state lottery tickets." *Sovetskie anekdoty*, 47; also Karachevtsev, *Dlia nekuriashchikh*, 139.

Иностранный корреспондент видит у хлебного магазина в Москве длинную очередь. Спрашивает советского гида:

—Что это за очередь?

—Это? ...Вы читали, вчера объявлен новый заём. Вот люди и спешат подписаться. Может не хватить на всех...

A foreign correspondent notices a long line outside a Moscow bread store. He asks his Soviet guide:

—What's that line for?

—That? Er, haven't you read that there was a new state bond issue announced yesterday? This is a line of people wanting to sign up. They're worried that there may not be enough bonds for everyone....[15]

☆ ☆ ☆

Иностранец с удивлением спрашивает советского коммуниста:

—Как вы так ловко делаете, что у вас все добровольно подписываются на заём.

—Все дело в подходе—вот у вас кошка не станет есть горчицу, а у нас ест.

—Как так.

—Помазать горчицей у кошки под хвостом—съест «добровольно».

A foreigner asks a Soviet communist with astonishment:

—How do you get everyone to voluntarily sign up for state bonds so easily?

—It's all in the approach. In your country, I bet you also can't get a cat to eat mustard, but we can.

—How's that?

—If you spread the mustard under the cat's tail, he'll lick it off "voluntarily."[16]

☆ ☆ ☆

Один еврей приехал в Москву по делу в госучреждение. Целый день посылали его от одного стола к другому. Ничего не добившись, он выходит из учреждения и раздраженно говорит своему приятелю:

—Это публичный дом какой-то!

Тот обиделся:

—Как ты смеешь так говорить?! Я в старое время в Одессе сам держал публичный дом, так там же был порядок!

—Ну, а теперь почему ты не держишь?

A Jew comes to Moscow to take care of some business at a state institution. All day long, he's sent from one office to another. Failing to get anything done, he leaves the building and exclaims in annoyance to one of his acquaintances:

—What a whorehouse!

His acquaintance takes offense.

—How dare you say such a thing! In the good old days, I ran a brothel in Odessa and we did everything there in an orderly fashion.

—So why did you give it up?

—Times have changed. Now they

---

[15] A variant of this joke is recounted as if it really happened in HPSSS, no. 97, schedule A, vol. 7, 28.

[16] An informant alludes to a variant of this joke in HPSSS, no. 30, schedule A, vol. 4, 17; for another version, see no. 2, schedule A, vol. 1, 20.

—Времена изменились. Теперь зададут норму, а если её не выдержишь, скажут ложись сам и выполняй промфинплан.

assign your organization a norm, and if it doesn't get fulfilled on time, you have get down on all fours and fulfill it yourself.

В Советском Союзе, как известно, ко всякому названию власть стремится пристегнуть прилагательное «красный»: Колхоз «Красный Пахарь», Завод «Красный Октябрь», Столовая «Красная Звезда» и т.п. Одна кустарно-промысловая артель, вырабатывающая синьку, называлась… «Красная Синька».

As is well known, in the Soviet Union they try to add the adjective "Red" to everything. There's a "Red Plowman" Collective Farm, a "Red October" Factory, a "Red Banner" Cafeteria, etc. One small industrial-handicraft concern that makes chemicals for brightening fabric is even called… "Red Bleach."

Everyday Life

Amid the celebratory propaganda surrounding collectivization, industrialization, Stakhanovite labor enthusiasm, and Five-Year Plan productivity targets, 180 million Soviet citizens trudged through an everyday existence that was considerably less heroic and triumphant. Along the way, they grumbled about a stunning array of complaints that complicated their daily lives, from overcrowded housing and public transport to rationing and long queues for basic necessities. Equally galling was the stifling officialese (*shtamp*) of Soviet mass culture, the careerism of party bureaucrats and the sycophancy of the creative intelligentsia.

While many of these expressions of discontent are interesting as historical artifacts of the era, they are also worth examining on account of the language in which they were expressed. After all, as sarcastic as they are, the jokes almost always rely on vocabulary and metaphors popularized by the state itself. Why would ordinary people choose to vent their anger and frustration in such orthodox terms? One possible explanation for this curious phenomenon stems from the pervasiveness of official sloganeering, analytical categories and cultural values in the state-sponsored mass culture of the 1930s. Stephen Kotkin, for instance, argues that this rhetoric was ubiquitous enough to reach hegemonic proportions, forcing even the most embittered to "speak Bolshevik" when expressing their discontent.[1] Alternately, this vocabulary and imagery can be seen as an intrinsic part of the Stalin era's culture of political humor, inasmuch as many of the jokes of the 1930s were based on the imitation, ridicule, and subversion of official "discourse." The presence of sarcasm and satire in these orthodox-sounding jokes, in other words, points as much to Soviet jokesters' individualism and capacity for critical thinking as it does to the hegemonic power of the regime's rhetoric.

Как Вы относитесь к советской власти?	What sort of relationship do you have to Soviet power?
Первый ответ:	First answer:
—Как к собственной жене: не люблю, но терплю.	—The same as I do with my own wife: I don't love her, but I put up with her.[2]

---

[1] Kotkin, *Magnetic Mountain*, chap. 5.

[2] For variants, see Lyons, *Moscow Carousel*, 327; HPSSS, no. 610, schedule B, vol. 20, 3.

Второй ответ:

—Как к собственной жене: немножко люблю, немножко боюсь, и страсть как хочется другой.

Second answer:

—The same as I do with my own wife: I love her a bit, fear her a bit, and desperately long for a different one.

Айсора, чистильщика сапог спрашивает клиент:

—Как тебе нравится Советская власть?

—Хороший советский власть, очень хороший, жаль только, что такой длинный....

An *Aisor*, a bootblack from the Caucasus, is asked by a client:

—What do you think about Soviet power?

—Soviet power is good, very good. It's just too bad it has to go on for so long.

Какая разница между матом и диаматом?

Матом кроют, а диаматом прикрывают. И то и другое—мощное оружие в руках пролетариата.

What's the difference between a diatribe and the Marxist dialectic?[3]

A diatribe lets you set people straight while the dialectic allows you to spin them in circles. Both are powerful weapons in the hands of the proletariat.

Один еврей, заполняя анкету, в графе о партийности написал «ВКП(б)». У него спрашивают:

—Что это Вы там написали? Вы же беспартийный!

—Я так и указал. ВКП(б) значит: Вроде Как Партийный, в скобках— Беспартийный.

While filling out a form, a Jew writes "ACP(b)" under "party affiliation." He's asked:

—Why did you write that? You're not a party member!

—And that's what I wrote. ACP(b) stands for: "Approximately Communist Party, but...."

Редактор провинциальной газеты исправляет заголовок над заметкой о несчастных случаях с автобусом. Вместо «Автобусы не должны давить людей» пишет: «Автобусы не должны давить пролетариев».

The editor of a provincial newspaper corrected the headline of a story on bus accidents. In the place of "Busses Must Not Run People Over," he wrote "Busses Must Not Run Proletarians Over."[4]

---

[3] In Russian this word play relies on the similarity between "*mat*" and "*diamat*." "*Mat*" is both the abbreviation for "materialism" and a term for a particularly obscene type of swearing. "*Diamat*," or "dialectical materialism," is a complex part of Marxist theory that few Soviets ever really understood.

[4] For a related joke about censorship, see *Sovetskie anekdoty*, 35.

⁂ ⁂ ⁂

Похороны члена Политбюро были обставлены с большой пышностью. Еврей интересуется у распорядителя:

—Скажите, пожалуйста, сколько стоют эти похороны?

—Сто тысяч рублей.

—Ой-ой-ой! Да я бы Вам за пять тысяч всё Политбюро похоронил.

The funeral of a Politburo member was conducted with great pomp and circumstance. A Jew asks the person in charge:

—Excuse me, how much did this funeral cost?

—A hundred thousand rubles.

—Goodness! You know, for five thousand, I'd have gladly buried the entire Politburo.[5]

⁂ ⁂ ⁂

Иностранный турист, изучающий русский язык, осматривает Москву. У кремлёвской стены ему показывают место, где похоронен Киров. Иностранец понимающе замечает:

—А… вот, где собака зарыта.

A foreign tourist studying Russian is taken for a tour around Moscow. At the Kremlin wall, he is shown Kirov's memorial plaque. Nodding his head, he replies awkwardly:

—Ah, so this is where all your bodies are buried.[6]

⁂ ⁂ ⁂

В райвоенкомате выясняется, что один из призываемых—глухонемой. Проверяли его всеми способами. Около уха стреляли—глазом не моргнул. Решили забраковать. Глухонемой уходит. Вслед за ним выходит один член комиссии, догоняет его в коридоре и, положив руку на плечо, спрашивает участливо:

—И давно это с тобой, хлопец, случилось?

—Месяца два уже….

At a local recruiting office, one of the draftees claims to be a deaf mute. They run him through all sorts of tests. A gun is even fired next to his ear and he doesn't blink an eye. They decide to give him an exemption. As the deaf mute leaves the office, a member of the commission catches up to him in the corridor and asks him sympathetically:

—You poor guy… where did this happen to you?

—Oh, a couple of months ago…

⁂ ⁂ ⁂

---

[5] Variant: "A Jew stops a well-known communist at an ostentatious funeral and asks with amazement how much the whole thing is costing the state. 'Very expensive. I think it cost about one hundred thousand,' the communist answers with a touch of pride. The Jew's indignant answer: 'And what about the austerity campaign? For half that price, I could have buried the entire Central Committee. And with pleasure.'" *Sovetskie anekdoty*, 11; also Karachevtsev, *Dlia nekuriashchikh*, 145.

[6] For a NEP-era variant, see *Sovetskie anekdoty*, 76.

Советский коммунист по
возвращении из командировки из
США докладывал: «В Америке народ
доголодался до того, что ест собачье
мясо: на улице в киосках открыто
продают горячую собачину. В толпе
безработных, глазевших на
футбольную игру, один молодой
человек спросил свою спутницу, хочет
ли она собачины, и она ответила: „О,
да, я умираю от голода"».

After his return from a business trip to
America, a Soviet communist reports: "In
America, the people are hungry enough
to eat dog meat—they sell it openly on
the street. I saw how a young man
watching a football game with a group of
unemployed workers asked his girlfriend
whether she wanted a hot dog. She
replied, 'Yes please, I'm starving to
death.'"

☆ ☆ ☆

После убийства Горького,
организованного Сталиным,
официальная советская критика
твердила, что «Максим Горький создал
эпоху в советской литературе».

Один советский литературовед
предложил назвать эту эпоху
«максимально-горькой».

After Stalin had Gor'kii[7] eliminated,
Soviet literary critics declared that
"Maksim Gor'kii created a whole epoch
in Soviet literature."

A Soviet academic specialist proposed
to refer to the epoch as "Maximally
Gory."[8]

☆ ☆ ☆

На эстраде висит портрет Сталина,
под ним—бюст Сталина. Докладчик
рассказывает про Сталина. Хор
исполняет «песню о Сталине». Артисты
декламируют оды и стихи в честь
Сталина. Что это такое?

Вечер, посвящённый памяти
Пушкина.

At a theater, a portrait of Stalin hangs
above the stage and below it stands a
bust of Stalin. A speaker talks about
Stalin. A chorus sings "The Song of
Stalin."[9] Artists recite odes and poems
about Stalin. What's going on?

An evening dedicated to the memory
of A. S. Pushkin.[10]

☆ ☆ ☆

По случаю 100-летия со дня смерти
Пушкина был объявлен всесоюзный

On the occasion of the 100th
commemoration of Pushkin's death, an

---

[7] Maksim Gor'kii (1868–1936), a prominent left-leaning novelist and short-story writer who, despite rumors to the contrary, probably died of natural causes.

[8] For a variant, see Sokolova, "Strana moego detstva," 366.

[9] "Pesnia o Staline," by A. Aleksandrov and S. Alymov, 1937.

[10] A. S. Pushkin (1799–1837), a nobleman, author and poet, who was co-opted by the USSR during the 100th commemoration of his death in 1937. He was venerated as a Soviet state hero and an anticipator of Socialist Realism. For a related joke, see HPSSS, no. 102, schedule B, vol. 14, 11.

конкурс проектов памятника великому поэту.

Из нескольких сотен проектов жюри приняло только один. Он выглядит так: с томиком Пушкина в руках в кресле сидит... Сталин.

all-union competition was announced to design a monument to the great poet.

The jury picked only one from the hundreds of proposals: there, sitting in a chair, reading from a volume of Pushkin, was... Stalin.[11]

Армянская загадка:

—Кто самый главный, в Кремле сидит, с буквы Е начинается.

   —Енукидзе?

—Нет.

   —Ежов?

—Нет.

   —Емельян Ярославский?

—Нет.

   —Кто же?

   —Е.. ... . Сталин!

An Armenian joke:

—Who's the most important fellow in the Kremlin whose name begins with "M"?

   —Molotov?[12]

—No.

   —Mikoian?[13]

—No.

   —Malenkov?[14]

—No.

   —Well, who then?

   —That Motherfucker Stalin.

Для привлечения публики один театр поместил на своей афише следующую приписку:

—Лучшим номером нашей программы будет последний. Кому он не понравится, может получить деньги обратно.

Публика повалила в театр. Кассирша, мило улыбаясь, сидела в кассе.

Последним номером была исполнена... «песня о Сталине».

In order to advertise a variety show, a theater put up the following sign:

—Our performance concludes with the best piece on the program. There's a money-back guarantee for anyone who is not fully satisfied.

The theater filled to overflowing, but the cashier just sat in her booth, relaxed and smiling. After all, the last number to be performed was... "The Song of Stalin."

---

[11] One related NEP-era joke held that after St. Petersburg was renamed Leningrad, some believed that the party would soon retitle *The Collected Works of Pushkin* as *The Collected Works of Lenin*. Insofar as St. Petersburg had been known colloquially as "Piter," another joke alleged that the planet Jupiter would soon be renamed "Ju-Lenin." See "Sovetskie anekdoty," 56; also *Sovetskie anekdoty*, 31.

[12] V. M. Molotov (1890–1986), an Old Bolshevik and party hierarch.

[13] A. I. Mikoian (1895–1978), an Old Bolshevik commissar in charge of the food industry.

[14] G. M. Malenkov (1902–88), an Old Bolshevik and party hierarch.

☆ ☆ ☆

Два мальчика, американский и советский, разговаривают:
—У нас есть шоколад.
—А у нас есть Сталин.
—Подумаешь, Сталина мы тоже могли бы иметь.
—А тогда у вас не было бы шоколада.

Two boys, one American and one Soviet, are having a conversation:
—We have chocolate.
—And we have Stalin.
—We could have Stalin too.
—But then you wouldn't have chocolate.

☆ ☆ ☆

Загадка:
Однажды Сталин с членами Политбюро и со всеми своими приближенными ехал на пароходе по Волге. Внезапно пароход начал тонуть. Если пароход мгновенно потонет, кто спасётся?
Отгадка:
Народы СССР.

A riddle:
Imagine that Stalin, the members of the Politburo, and their whole entourage are aboard a steamer on the Volga. Suddenly, the steamer begins to sink. If the steamer were to go down in an instant, who would be saved?
Answer: All the peoples of the USSR.

☆ ☆ ☆

Вопрос: Как живётся под советской властью?
Первый ответ:
—Как в автобусе: одни сидят, а другие трясутся.
Второй ответ:
—Как на океанском пароходе: необъятные горизонты, тошнит, и деваться некуда.
Третий ответ:
—Хуже, чем вчера, лучше, чем завтра.

A question: What's it like to live under Soviet power?
First answer:
—It's like in a crowded bus: some struggle to get out while others just stand there, shaking.
Second answer:
—It's like on an ocean liner: the horizon stretches out forever, you're nauseous, and there's no way off.
Third answer:
—Every day's worse than the day before but better than the day after.[15]

---

[15] For variants, see HPSSS, no. 610, schedule B, vol. 20, 3.

FIGURE 25. Workers in the offices of Leningrad's Russian Diesel Plant

✩ ✩ ✩

Еврей рассказывает знакомому:
—Детки мои, слава Богу, устроились хорошо. Хаим—инженер, Сарочка—врач, Абрам—бухгалтер. Только один Лёва непутёвый—сидит в Америке безработным. Хотя... правда, если бы он нам не присылал посылок, то мы бы все здесь с голоду поздыхали....

A Jew tells a friend:
—My children, thank God, are pretty well set. Khaim is an engineer, Sara is a doctor and Abraham is a bookkeeper. Only Lev is unlucky—he's stuck in America without a job. I guess I should say, though, that if he weren't sending us care packages, we'd have all starved to death by now....

✩ ✩ ✩

Два советских гражданина разговаривают:
—Как ты думаешь, какой национальности были Адам и Ева?
—Несомненно они были советскими гражданами: носить у них было нечего, жрать было только одно яблоко и жили они в раю.

Two Soviets are talking:
—What do you think was Adam and Eve's nationality?
—Soviet, no doubt. They had nothing to wear, only a single apple to eat, and thought they were living in paradise.

СССР—страна радости.
Влез в трамвай—радость. Добрался в очереди до хлеба—радость. Удалось достать газету—радость. Сплошная радость!

The USSR is a land of happiness. You squeeze aboard a tram—happiness. You get a bit of bread after standing in line—happiness. You get ahold of a newspaper—happiness. There's happiness everywhere you look![16]

☆ ☆ ☆

О ленинградских трамваях: «Стою на одной ноге и то на чужой.»

There's a saying about the Leningrad trams: "I'm standing on only one foot and it's not even my own."

☆ ☆ ☆

Скоро в київских трамваях
Будут говорити:
Злазьте з мене, громодяне,
Бо мені сходити.[17]

Soon in the Kievan trams,
You'll be hearing on every street:
Comrade, this is my stop,
It's time you got off my feet.

☆ ☆ ☆

В Москве два солдата входят в трамвай. Задний, налегая плечом:
—Ты, Ваня, проси вежливо, а я поднажму.

In Moscow, two soldiers are getting aboard a tram. The second one leans up against the first with his shoulder and says:
—Vania, ask those in front of you to make room politely and I'll shove you in from behind.

☆ ☆ ☆

В советском городе—мясная лавка. Дверь открыта, на полках лежит мясо, но покупателей почему-то нет. К лавке подходит женщина и не решается войти. Продавец:
—Гражданочка, почему не покупаете?
Женщина растерянно:
—А я... жду, когда очередь соберётся....

At a Soviet butcher's shop, the door is open and there is meat on the counter, but there aren't any customers. A woman comes up to the shop but hesitates before entering. The salesman says:
—Lady, why're you just standing there?
The woman responds nervously:
—Er... I'm waiting for a line to form.

---

[16] Variant: "There is a joke about the Soviet Union being the happiest country in the world: 'If you get 100 grams of butter you are lucky; if you manage to sit down in a streetcar you are lucky; if you manage to get anything else you're also lucky... thus there are more opportunities to be lucky than anywhere else in the world.'" HPSSS, no. 1693, schedule A, vol. 36, 31.

[17] Original in Ukrainian.

✱ ✱ ✱

Одна провинциальная газета проводила кампанию «за лучшее обслуживание трудящихся». Среди разных заголовков над заметками был и такой: «Кладбища—ближе к трудящимся».

A provincial newspaper article announced a campaign to promote "Superior Service for the Working Class." Among the many headings in the piece was the following: "Let's Make Cemeteries More Accessible to the Working Class!"

✱ ✱ ✱

Одному усердному служащему удалось получить записку на ж.д. станцию о том, чтобы ему выдали «билет по брони без очереди». На станции он суёт записку кассиру. Тот указывает:

—Станьте, пожалуйста, вон в ту очередь.

—Позвольте, но ведь там сказано «без очереди».

—Та очередь как раз и есть для тех, у кого записки «без очереди».

A zealous office worker manages to get a certificate entitling him to book a train ticket without standing in line. At the station, however, the cashier takes one look at the certificate and sends him to the back of the line.

—Wait your turn, please.

—But this says that I don't have to wait in line.

—This is the line for everyone who doesn't have to wait in line.

✱ ✱ ✱

Экскурсия колхозников из отдалённых провинций осматривает Москву. Экскурсовод рассказывает им... о «достижениях», о «заботе о человеке», о «возросших потребностях советских людей» и об «изобилии товаров ширпотреба».

Один из колхозников:

—Товарищ начальник, а я вот вчера целый день ходил по улицам и не видел того, о чём Вы рассказываете....

Экскурсовод раздраженно:

—Ты бы поменьше по улицам шлялся, побольше бы газеты читал!

Some collective farmers from deep in the provinces were taking a tour of Moscow. Their guide tells them about all the various "accomplishments": the "attention to people's needs," "the growing consumption habits of the Soviet people," and the "surplus of consumer goods."

One of the collective farmers pipes up:

—Comrade boss, I spent all of yesterday walking around Moscow and I didn't see what you are describing.

The tour guide responds angrily:

—Well, I would advise you to spend less time fooling around on the street and more time reading the newspaper.[18]

[18] Variant: "There was a joke which dates back to 1927 and 1928 which is as follows: The Odessa Raicom [sic, Raikom] Party Secretary was saying that the regime was

В советском цирке выходит клоун, обвешанный со всех сторон продуктами: колбасами, сырами, хлебом, маслом и т. п. Он важно расхаживает по арене минуту, другую, третью, ничего не говоря. Кто-то из публики не выдерживает:

—Сколько ещё времени вы будете молчать?

—Я?! Мне незачем кричать—у меня всё есть, а вот сколько времени вы будете молчать?..

At the Soviet circus, a clown appears on stage weighed down with all kinds of food: sausages, cheese, bread, butter, etc. He proudly walks through the arena, saying nothing. A minute passes, and then another. Finally, someone from the audience yells out:

—How much longer are you going to stay silent?

—Me? I don't have any reason to say anything: I have everything that I need. How much longer are *you* going to stay silent?

Одна старушка каждый день заходила в газетный киоск, смотрела первую страницу «Известий» и молча уходила. Продавец спросил её:

—И чего ты, бабушка, каждый день ищешь в «Известиях»?

—Жду всё известия об одной смерти.

—Так ведь это на четвёртой странице печатается….

—Нет, сыночек, та смерть, которую я жду, будет на первой странице пропечатана.

An old woman came up to a newspaper stand every day, took a look at the first page of *Izvestiia*, and then left without saying a word. The newspaper boy finally asks her one day:

—Granny, what are you looking for in *Izvestiia* every day?

—I'm waiting for an obituary.

—But then you should be looking on the fourth page, where they're usually listed.

—No sonny, the one I'm waiting for will be printed on the first page.[19]

—Куда девалось масло?
—Растаяло «под солнцем Сталинской конституции».

—Where did all the butter go?
—It must have melted "in the bright rays of the Stalin Constitution."

★ ★ ★

doing great things. The secretary said that the regime had erected a dock in the harbor. Another fellow, a critic, said that he went down to the harbor and that he had not seen this new dock. The secretary retorted: 'Comrade, you don't read the newspaper.'" HPSSS, no. 32, schedule A, vol. 4, 54; also no. 11, schedule A, vol. 2, 31.

[19] Variant in HPSSS, no. 1007, schedule A, vol. 31, 69.

FIGURE 26. M. I. Tukhachevskii

Тухачевский сказал как-то:

«Замечательная черта британской королевской армии заключается в том, что к её руководству не лезет ни один сыщик из Скотланд-Ярда, а сапожники допускаются только до интендантских складов».

Tukhachevskii[20] once said:

—The best thing about the British Royal Army is that they've never allowed Scotland Yard into the high command and don't allow their cobblers past the warehouses.[21]

Пропагандно-лирические «песенки Дунаевского», имевшие большой успех в СССР и принесшие ордена композитору, как известно основаны на мелодиях, заимствованных и переделанных из старой музыки.

«С миру по нотке — Дунаевскому орден».

Propaganda songs by Dunaevskii[22] were very popular in the USSR and earned their composer awards, even though it was well known that they were based on melodies that he had adapted from older music. It was said that "Dunaevskii earns his medals by the note."

---

[20] M. I. Tukhachevskii (1895–1937), a Red Army marshal purged during the Great Terror.

[21] A reference to rumors that the Red Army high command was rife with secret police informants; the cobbler comment is an oblique barb at Stalin, whose father was a bootmaker.

[22] I. O. Dunaevskii (1900–55), a composer credited with tunes from movies such as *The Happy-Go-Lucky Guys* (*Vselye rebiata*, G. V. Aleksandrov, 1934), *Circus* (*Tsirk*, Aleksandrov, 1936), and *Volga-Volga* (Aleksandrov, 1938). The latter two earned him Stalin prizes in 1940 and 1951.

В связи с проведением кампании против грубого натурализма, трюкачества в искусстве и сумбура в музыке, партком одного зоосада наметил к исключению:

Носорога—за грубый натурализм,
Жирафа—за трюкачество,
Зебру—за сумбур в природе.

In connection with the campaign against vulgar naturalism, artistic excess, and cacophony in music,[23] the party committee of a public zoo announced several expulsions:

the rhino, for vulgar naturalism,
the giraffe, for artistic excess,
and the zebra, for cacophony.[24]

☆ ☆ ☆

Сталинский пропагандный подхалим, так называемый «украинский драматург» Корнейчук, хвалится:

—Я огонь вложил в мою драму!
Читатель:
—Лучше бы наоборот....

Korneichuk,[25] the Stalinist propaganda sycophant and so-called "Ukrainian playwright," once boasted:

—I put fire into my plays!
The reader thinks to himself:
—It'd be better if it were the other way around.

☆ ☆ ☆

Перед введением Сталинской Конституции счастливые советские граждане недоумённо спрашивали друг друга:

—Дошли ли мы уже до социализма или будет ещё хуже?

Before the introduction of the "Stalin Constitution,"[26] the joyous Soviet citizens asked one another incredulously:

—Have we reached socialism yet or will it get even worse?

☆ ☆ ☆

Обычный вопрос в день выборов в Москве:

—Иван Иванович, Вами уже выбирали?

A typical question on election day in Moscow:

—Ivan Ivanovich, has your vote already been cast for you?

☆ ☆ ☆

---

[23] Reference to the "muddle instead of music" scandal surrounding Dmitrii Shostakovich's *Lady Macbeth of Mtsensk District*—see "Sumbur vmesto muziki," *Pravda*, 28 January 1936, p. 3.

[24] For a variant, see Sokolova, "Iz starykh tetradei, 1935–1937," 353.

[25] A. O. Korneichuk (1905–72), a Ukrainian playwright best known for *The Squadron's Fate* (*Gibel' eskadry*, 1933), *Bogdan Khmel'nitskii* (1939), and *Front* (1942).

[26] The "Stalin" Constitution was promulgated in 1936, ostensibly to provide a social contract for the newly socialist economy.

FIGURE 27. Coat of arms of the USSR

На политзанятиях пропагандист втолковывает рабочим статью 143 Великой Сталинской Конституции: «Государственный герб Союза Советских Социалистических Республик состоит из серпа и молота на земном шаре, изображённом в лучах солнца и обрамлённом колосьями, с надписью на языках союзных республик: «Пролетарии всех стран, соединяйтесь».

Рабочим тема понравилась. После политзанятий, идя домой, рабочие вспоминали пройденное:

Слева молот, справа серп,
Это наш советский герб.
Хочешь жни, хочешь куй,
Всё равно получишь….» (Одно и то же).

In a political study circle, a propagandist explained to some workers the nature of Article 143 of the Stalin Constitution: "The coat of arms of the USSR is made up of a hammer and sickle rising over the globe, sparkling in the sun's rays, framed with sheaves of grain, and labeled 'Workers of the World, Unite!'" in the languages of the republics.

The workers liked this subject. Walking home after class, they thought over what they had learned:

Hammer to the left, sickle to the right,
Our coat of arms is quite a sight.
Do you want to hammer? Do you want to reap?
You're fucked either way, so don't utter a peep.

★ ★ ★

Взвод вышел в поле на тактические занятия. Наступает час политзанятий. Командир взвода, глядя на часы, с досадой:

Сержант Петров, расскажи ребятам… что такое сицилизма и на кой хрен она нам нужна.

A platoon is in the field for tactical exercises but it's interrupted by the obligatory "political studies" hour. The platoon comander looks at his watch impatiently and barks:

—Sergeant Petrov, explain to the lads what Marx's theory of syphilism is and why the fuck they should care.

✯ ✯ ✯

Советский коммунист, показав иностранцу все «наши достижения», говорит:

—Ну, теперь Вы видите, что можно построить социализм в одной стране.

Иностранец мнётся:

—Можно то можно, да кто в такой стране станет жить?

A Soviet communist finishes showing a foreigner all of "our accomplishments" and boasts:

—So as you can see, it's possible to build socialism in one country after all.

The foreigner mutters to himself:

—Well, of course it's possible, but who would want to live there?[27]

✯ ✯ ✯

Перед витриной московского магазина с гастрономическими продуктами и астрономическими ценами остановился старый учитель со школьниками:

—Смотрите, детки, как ели ваши предки до первой пятилетки.

An elderly teacher and his students stop in front of the window of a Moscow store where food is being displayed at astronomical prices:

—Look, children, this is what your ancestors ate before the first Five-Year Plan.[28]

✯ ✯ ✯

Один советский профессор смотрит на бананы, выставленные в витрине коммерческого магазина:

—Да,… живём как в Африке.

—Почему?—спросил кто-то.

—Едим бананы и ходим голыми.

A Soviet professor looks at some bananas laid out in the display window of a commercial store.[29]

—Hmmm…. It's almost as if we live in Africa.

Someone asks:

—What do you mean?

—We're eating bananas and walking around naked.[30]

✯ ✯ ✯

---

[27] For variants, see Karachevtsev, *Dlia nekuriashchikh,*135–36; Lyons, *Moscow Carousel,* 329.

[28] For a variant, see HPSSS, no. 5, schedule A, vol. 1, 18. According to a postwar interview, "People frequently go and stand in front of these stores and look at the display of all the food in the window; we have a saying about this, as follows: *Nagliadnoe posobie po zaochnomu pitaniiu* [Visual aides of food consumption in absentia]." HPSSS, no. 446, schedule B, vol. 13, 34.

[29] A store where goods in short supply were sold at high prices to generate additional revenue for the state.

[30] For a variant, see HPSSS, no. 127, schedule A, vol. 10, 36–37.

Было предложено исключить из русской азбуки букву М, т.к. нет ни масла, ни молока, ни мяса, ни муки, ни мыла....

Предложение, однако, было отвергнуто, потому, что есть Микоян—Нарком пищепромышленности.

Someone suggested that the letter "M" be stricken from the Russian alphabet, insofar as there wasn't any margarine, milk, or meat....

This proposal wasn't enacted because of Mikoian, Minister of Food Industry.[31]

—Вы знаете, вчера Сталин сказал: «жить стало лучше, жить стало веселее».

—Слышал. Но он не сказал кому.

—Did you hear? Stalin said yesterday that "life has gotten better, life has gotten more joyous."

—Yeah, I heard. But he didn't say for whom.[32]

Высокое партначальство из центра инспектирует психиатрическую лечебницу где-то в провинции. Начальство заходит в одну палату. Все сумасшедшие встают и орут в один голос:

—Жить стало лучше, жить стало веселее!

Начальство довольно—лозунг доведён даже до сумасшедших. Но... начальство заметило, что в углу стоял невзрачный человек и молчал. Начальство подходит к нему:

—А почему Вы не кричали «жить стало лучше?

—Простите, я не сумасшедший, я служащий.

Central party officials arrived at a psychiatric institution somewhere in the provinces for an inspection. When the bosses went into one of the wards, all the patients stood at attention and shouted in unison:

—Life has gotten better, life has gotten more joyous!

The bosses were satisfied that even these patients knew the slogan. But they did notice that one nondescript fellow standing in the corner hadn't said a word. The bosses walk up to him:

—Why didn't you shout out "Life has gotten better?"

—Er, I'm not crazy... I work here.[33]

* * *

---

[31] A variant of this joke apparently resulted in the arrest of at least one jokester during the 1930s—see HPSSS, no. 396, schedule A, vol. 20, 10.

[32] This famous line stems from a speech of Stalin's in November 1935. See I. V. Stalin, "Rech' na I vsesoiuznom soveshchanii Stakhanovtsev," *Pravda*, 22 November 1935, p. 1. Telling this joke is discussed in HPSSS, no. 455, schedule A, vol. 23, 73.

[33] For a variant, see HPSSS, no. 446, schedule B, vol. 13, 73.

Одной старушке партком предложил выступить на собрании и выразить благодарность вождю за счастье, которое, разумеется, переполняет её жизнь. Старушка вспомнила развешанные на улицах лозунги: «Спасибо дорогому Сталину за нашу счастливую жизнь», взошла на трибуну и сказала:

—Спасибо счастливому Сталину за нашу дорогую жизнь.

Это были её последние слова.

An elderly woman was asked by her party committee to give a speech at a conference where she would thank the great leader for the happiness that had made her life worth living. She recalled seeing on the street a poster with the slogan, "Thank you dear Stalin for our happy lives" and made her way to the tribune, where she said:

—Thank you happy Stalin for our dear lives.

Those were the last words she ever uttered.

Один гражданин заходит в магазин купить какую-нибудь картину для своей комнаты. Продавец показывает ему всего две картины, имеющиеся в магазине: групповой портрет Политбюро и Ленин в мавзолее.

—Неужели у вас ничего иного нет?

—Ничего. Возьмите эти чудесные портреты вождей!

—Дда… не плохи, но я хотел бы вот этот групповой портретик (показывает на Политбюро) иметь в этой позе (указывает на Ленина).

A Soviet citizen goes into a store to buy a picture to hang in his room. A salesman shows him the only two in the store: a group portrait of the Politburo and Lenin in the mausoleum.

—Are you sure you don't have anything else?

—No, nothing else. Take these wonderful pictures of the party leaders.

—Well, they're not bad. But I'd prefer a picture of this group (pointing to the Politburo) in that pose (pointing to Lenin).[34]

Учительница раздала трём детям в школе портреты Сталина и на следующий день спрашивает их, что они с портретами сделали.

—Я повесил портрет на стене прямо против двери, чтобы все входящие его видели,—сказал один мальчик.

—Я повесил в углу, где раньше были

One day, a school teacher gives portraits of Stalin to three students in her class. The next day, she asks them what they'd done with them.

—I hung the portrait directly opposite our front door at home, so that all those entering will see it.

—I hung mine in the corner where our

---

[34] For variants, see Karachevtsev, *Dlia nekuriashchikh,* 131; Lyons, *Moscow Carousel,* 325. A variant from the 1920s has a Communist Party member asking a Jew:

—Say, Barzhanskii, who would you like to see in Lenin's place?

—Oh, I'd like all of you in Lenin's place.

"Sovetskie anekdoty," 55; *Sovetskie anekdoty,* 15; see also 57.

иконы, — сказал другой мальчик.

Третий мальчик молчал.

Учительница:

—Ну, а ты, Петя, куда ты портрет повесил?

—Никуда — замялся Петя.

—Как никуда?! Почему?

—Да наша семья живёт в середине комнаты, а у стен живут четыре других семьи.

icons used to be.

The third boy remains silent. The teacher asks him:

—And you, Petia, where did you hang your portrait?

—I didn't hang it anywhere.

—What? Why not?

—There was nowhere to hang it.

—What do you mean nowhere?

—Well, our family lives in the middle of a room. The walls belong to the four other families who live there with us.

В одном лекционном зале в Москве советский художник руководил размещением портретов вождей. Указывая на портрет Сталина, рабочие спрашивают:

—Этого куда?

—Этого повесить.

—А этого? — спрашивают рабочие, указывая на портрет Молотова.

—А этого к стенке поставить.

In a Moscow lecture hall, an artist is coordinating the arrangement of the leaders' portraits. Pointing to a portrait of Stalin, the workers ask:

—Where should Stalin go?

—String him up.

Pointing to a picture of Molotov, the workers ask:

—And Molotov?

—Up against the wall.[35]

В окнах многих магазинов в СССР выставляются портреты вождей. В одной аптеке заведующий выставил портреты Сталина и Молотова. Прохожие с удовольствием читали не убранную под ними надпись: «Свежие пиявки».

Many stores in the USSR displayed portraits of the Soviet leadership in their windows. The director of a pharmacy put up pictures of Stalin and Molotov. Passers-by noticed with delight that he forgot to remove a sign in the window that read "fresh leeches."

---

[35] Variant: according to the deputy director of the Kama River steamship political department, in February 1935 a candidate party member named Esin made disrespectful comments about Kirov and Stalin and added, gesturing toward the general secretary's portrait: "It'd be great to hang them along with Lenin on a single wire" (*Vot by ikh povesit' na odnoi provolke vmeste s Leninym*). RGASPI f. 17, op. 120, d. 174, l. 68; also HPSSS, no. 53, schedule A, vol. 5, 10; no. 305, schedule A, vol. 15, 18; no. 53, schedule B, vol. 1, 15.

В магазине Осоавиахима гражданин покупает парашют. С некоторой подозрительностью осматривает знаменитое «качество советской продукции» и сомневается:

—А вдруг он не раскроется?

Продавщица вежливо:

—Ну, тогда придёте, мы Вам переменим.

A man goes into the Osoaviakhim store,[36] wanting to buy a parachute. He looks with suspicion at the famous "Soviet Quality" tag and asks:

—And what if it doesn't open?

The shopgirl answers politely:

—Just bring it back and we'll exchange it for you.

Блатмейстер в Москве пытается попасть в кино бесплатно. Заходит к администратору:

—Друг, дай пару контрамарок,— говоритон небрежно, отворачивая полу пальто ипоказывая на груди знак, смахивающий накрупный орден.

—Контрамарки у нас отменены.

—Чёрт знает что! Я сейчас позвоню вКремль.

Снимает трубку, набирает какой-то номер.

—Дайте Молотова! Что? Спасибо. Вячик, что это у тебя в кино «Заря Революции» контрамарок не дают? Что? Сказать от твоего имени, чтобы дали.... Спасибо, дорогой!

Администратор заискивающе:

—Вы с Вашими высокими связями, может, мне поможете: попросили бы, чтобы мне этот телефон исправили— два месяца уже, как не работает....

A wheeler-and-dealer in Moscow once attempted to get into a movie theater for free. He walks up to the administrator, flashes his lapel pin as if it were a prominent medal, and then asks causally:

—Can I have a couple of passes, my good friend?

—We don't give out passes anymore.

—What the hell? Let me call the Kremlin.

He grabs the telephone and dials a number.

—Let me have Molotov. What? Okay, thank you. Hello, Viachik. Why isn't the "Dawn of the Revolution" Theater giving out passes any more? What? Shall I use your name when I ask for them? Thanks a lot!

The administrator stutters:

—Maybe with your big connections, you might be able to help me. Could you request that they fix that telephone you just used? It hasn't worked in two months....

В Ленинграде американец спрашивает советскую даму, как должен поступить иностранец, если он хочет завести

In Leningrad, an American asks a Soviet lady what a foreigner should do if he wants to go out on a date. Soviet

---

[36] Society for the Aid of National Defense and the Airplane and Chemical Industries (*Obshchestvo sodeistviia oborone, aviatsionnomu i khimicheskomu stroitel'stvu SSSR*), 1927–1948.

девушку. Советские женщины, мол, известны своим патриотизмом и недоступностью, да и неудобно же приставать на улице. Дама ответила:

—Очень просто: на каждом телефоне есть две кнопки А и Б. Нажмите любую и просите любой номер.

women, after all, are famous for their patriotism and unapproachability, making it awkward to try to meet someone on the street. The lady answers:

—You know, it's very simple. Every Soviet telephone has two buttons: A and B. Press either one and ask the operator for the first number that comes into your head.[37]

☆　☆　☆

Для того, чтобы изолировать иностранцев от советских женщин, Сталин открыл в Москве… публичный дом, который он скромно назвал «научно-исследовательским институтом любви». Иностранцы, знакомые с научно-исследовательскими учреждениями СССР, говорили так: · «Это—единственный институт, где не занимаются онанизмом».

In order to protect Soviet women in Moscow from foreigners, Stalin opened… a brothel, which he modestly called the "Scholarly Research Institute of Love." Foreigners acquainted with the USSR's other research institutions scoffed that this was "the only institute where people were not simply jerking off."

☆　☆　☆

Известно, что на советских политических докладах публика обычно дремлет, да и президиум одолевает сон. В такой нормальной обстановке докладчик, кончая своё выступление, патетически воскликнул:

—…враги народа хотели убить нашего любимого вождя, *товарища Сталина!*

Разбуженные упоминанием великого имени члены президиума вскочили и бешено зааплодировали….

It's well known that the Soviet public often drifted off during political speeches, as did the party presidium. Such was the case one day when a speaker, finishing his presentation, shouted out:

—…thus the enemies of the people aimed to kill our beloved leader, *Comrade Stalin!*

Awakened by the invocation of this great name, the members of the presidium jumped to their feet and furiously began to clap….

---

[37] Early Soviet telephones had two buttons, each of which would connect the caller to an operator. The implication here is that *any* Soviet woman would agree to a date with a foreigner.

The Great Terror

Between 1936 and 1938, rumors of conspiracies fomented by German, Polish, and Japanese secret agents or renegades like Trotskii triggered an explosion of popular fear and xenophobia in Soviet society. The show-trial confessions of Old Bolsheviks supposedly involved in these conspiracies fed the flames, as did reports of treachery throughout the Red Army high command. A firestorm of denunciation and arrest quickly spread to the mass level of society, terrorizing rank-and-file party members as well as teachers, engineers, and members of the Soviet elite.

Long a source of confusion, Stalin's purges appear to have been a preemptive strike against purported fifth columns and "unreliable elements" within the party and state bureaucracy, the armed forces and society as a whole. Such an explanation accounts not only for the arrest of many of Stalin's perceived rivals within the party ranks, but for the wholesale purge of certain ethnic minorities as well as social marginals, non-conformists, and recidivists.[1] This latter "prophylactic" round-up of former *kulaks*, black marketeers, prostitutes, and other "usual suspects" targeted "anti-social" groups perceived to be holdovers from the capitalist economy. In all, some 680,000 "enemies of the people" were executed between 1936 and 1938, while another three million were sent to GULag prison camps or exiled to the barren wastes of Siberia and the far north.[2]

Ordinary Soviets struggled in vain to make sense of the purges. Many seem to have accepted official accounts of treason in high places. Others believed that the purge was chiefly aimed at communists and Jews.[3] Still others expressed discomfort with such logical explanations, attributing the frenzy of bloodletting to Stalin's paranoiac insecurity or the murderous psychopathol-

---

[1] Ethnic minorities living in Soviet border regions—people of Korean, Finnish, Polish, and Bulgarian ancestry, for instance—were perceived to have divided loyalties and became some of the terror's least known victims.

[2] J. Arch Getty, Gabor T. Rittersporn, and V. N. Zemskov, "Victims of the Soviet Penal System in the Pre-War Years: A First Approach on the Basis of Archival Evidence," *American Historical Review* 98: 4 (1993): 1017–49.

[3] F. Beck and W. Godin, *Russian Purge and the Extraction of Confession*, trans. Eric Mosbacher and David Porter (New York: Viking Press, 1951), 146.

ogy of the NKVD and its leader, N. I. Ezhov.[4] Political jokes in circulation at the time depicted the waves of arrests as simultaneously systematic and random. Persecution was inevitable and resistance futile. Such naïve, hysterical, and internally inconsistent explanations at the grass roots level testify to ordinary Soviets' widespread confusion and their panicky search for a way to make sense of the Great Terror.

На партсъезде Сталин закончил свою речь словами:

—Итак, товарищи, выполним завет великого Ленина!

В этот момент Сталина вызвали к телефону:

—Сталин слушает.

—Говорит Ленин....

—Откуда Вы, Ильич, дорогой?..

—Об этом после, а пока скажи-ка, что это ты там за свинство без меня устроил?

Сталин бросил трубку и подозвал охрану:

—Найти и убрать этого врага народа.

At a party conference, Stalin concluded his speech with the words:

—And so, comrades, let us fulfill Lenin's testament.

Suddenly, the phone rings and Stalin is handed the receiver.

—This is Stalin.

—Stalin, this is Lenin....

—Where are you calling from, dear Il'ich?

—That can wait—first, tell me what all this swinishness is about that you've gone and done without me?

Stalin slams down the phone and calls to his guard:

—Find that enemy of the people and arrest him.

Разгневанный Сталин вызвал к себе Радека:

—Ты что это на меня анекдоты сочиняешь?! Даже осмеливаешься про то, что я—вождь мировой революции!

Радек:

—Товарищ Сталин, помилуй, ведь анекдота, что ты—вождь мировой революции, право же, никто не сочинял....

Furious, Stalin summons Radek to his office.

—What are you telling jokes about me for? You even dare to joke about me as the leader of the world revolution!

Radek replies:

—Comrade Stalin, forgive me, but no one's ever joked about you being leader of the world revolution.[5]

---

[4] The 1936–38 time period is referred to in Russian as the *ezhovshchina* (lit.: "the pernicious times of Ezhov").

[5] One former Soviet citizen went so far as to declare in 1951 that "Radek is the author of almost all the counter-revolutionary anecdotes which are told in the Soviet Union"; another claimed that he had been purged on account of his jokes about Stalin. Lyons recalls having heard the first of these rumors, although he treats it with much more

Трое заключённых встречаются в пересыльном лагере.

Первый:

—Сижу я с 1929 года за то, что назвал Карла Радека контрреволюцинером.

Второй:

—А я сижу с 1937 года за то, что сказал, что Карл Радек—не контрреволюционер.

Третий:

—А я, извините, сам Карл Радек....

Three prisoners meet at a transit camp. The first says:

—I've been in prison since 1929 for calling Karl Radek a counterrevolutionary.

The second replies:

—I've been here since 1938 for saying that Radek wasn't a conterrevolutionary.

The third interjects:

—And I'm sorry to say that I *am* Karl Radek.

Рыков от природы был заика. Во время его травли, организованной Сталиным, партийцы говорили:

—Рыков заикаться перестал.

—Вылечился?

—Какое! Ему и заикнуться не дают.

Rykov stuttered all his life. But during the show trial that Stalin organized in order to persecute him, party members observed to one-another:

—Rykov has stopped stuttering.

—Has he been cured?

—No. He's been forbidden to utter even a stutter.

Как только Сталин ликвидировал «оппозиции» и начал выдвигать на важные посты кавказских людей, все чистильщики сапог в Москве (айсоры) отказались чистить и сидели сложа руки.

Их спросили:

— Почему?

Они ответили:

—Ажидаем балших назначений.

After Stalin finished eliminating the "opposition" and began to move cadres from the Caucasus into major party posts, Moscow's bootblacks (the *Aisors*) all refused to do their work and just sat around with their legs crossed.

When people asked them what was going on, they answered (in heavily accented Russian):

—We're expecting major promotions.[6]

---

skepticism. See HPSSS, no. 149, schedule A, vol. 11, 41; no. 446, schedule B, vol. 13, 73; Lyons, *Moscow Carousel*, 322.

[6] Stalin's supposed promotion of Caucasians into the central party apparatus apparently referred to the advancement of G. K. Ordzhonikidze, Mikoian, A. S. Enukidze, and Kirov into high posts, misdated to the second half of the 1930s. According to popular wisdom, the *Aisors*, an ethnic group from the Caucasus, dominated the shoeshine trade in Moscow.

FIGURE 28. Workers chatting as they clean a piece of equipment

—Что слышно в Политбюро?
—Как всегда ничего, только запах изменился.
—Как так?
—Раньше пахло чесноком, а теперь шашлыком.

—What have you heard about the Politburo?
—Nothing much, as always, except that the smell has changed.
—What do you mean?
—Before, it smelled of garlic and now it's shishkebab.[7]

Все ночи напролёт работнички НКВД «трудились», арестовывая, пытая и убивая людей. Между собой стали «шутить».
—Что такое НКВД?
—Неизвестно Когда Вернёшься Домой.

NKVD agents spent every night hard at "work," arresting, torturing, and killing people. They sometimes "joked" among themselves:
—What does NKVD stand for?
—"Nobody Knew this Vocation was so Demanding."

Следователи советской тайной полиции, хорошо знающие их собственные методы, говорят так: «Был

Soviet secret police investigators who know their trade well say: "Get your man first and work out the charges later."

---

[7] This reference to cuisine refers to rumors that Stalin had replaced Jewish Politburo members with appointees from the Caucasus. A related joke: "Why is Stalin like Moses? Because Moses rid Egypt of the Jews and Stalin rid the Politburo of the Jews." HPSSS, no. 307, schedule A, vol. 16, 29; also *Sovetskie anekdoty*, 12.

бы человек, а статья найдётся».
Иллюстрация: педерасты осуждались
по ст. 58.10 «Агитация и пропаганда».

Homosexuals, for instance, could be
charged under Article 58/10, "Agitation
and Propaganda."

★ ★ ★

«Вход воспрещается» — такая надпись
висит на здании НКВД. Прохожий
еврей:
— Если бы они здесь повесили
«Добро пожаловать», я бы и тогда не
пошёл.

A sign saying "Entrance Forbidden"
hung outside NKVD headquarters. A
Jew passing by scoffs:
— I wouldn't go in there even if they
hung something up saying "Welcome!
Make yourself at home!"[8]

★ ★ ★

Два еврея проходят по Лубянке
(площадь, где находится НКВД в
Москве):
— Лёва, ты знаешь, какая разница
между Сталиным и ослом?
В этот момент из дверей НКВД
высовывается «чин» и подзывает
пальцем евреев к себе:
— А ну, подойди сюда, сказать тебе,
какая разница?
— Я, я ничего не сказал, нет, нет
никакой разницы....

Two Jews are walking on Lubianka
Square near the Moscow NKVD
headquarters.
— Lev, what's the difference between
Stalin and a donkey?
Suddenly, a policeman sticks his head
out of the building and points a finger at
the two Jews.
— Hey, you, come over here. Maybe
you'd like me to tell you the difference?
— Who, me? What difference? Did I say
there was a difference?

★ ★ ★

Самая длинная улица в мире — это
Литейный проспект в Ленинграде. Он
ведёт до самых Соловков и раньше, чем
через 3 года с него не возвращаются.

The longest street in the world is
Leningrad's Liteinyi Prospect. It leads
straight north to the Solovetskii islands
and if you go there, it'll take you at least
three years to return.[9]

★ ★ ★

Встречаются два зайца в поле:
— Отчего ты так бежишь, запыхался
даже?
— А ты разве не слышал, объявили,
что всех верблюдов будут кастрировать?

Two rabbits meet in a field.
— You're out of breath — what are you
running from?
— Haven't you heard? They've
announced that they're going to start

---

[8] For a variant, see Lyons, *Moscow Carousel*, 338.

[9] The Leningrad headquarters of the NKVD were located on Liteinyi Prospect and the
Solovetskii islands were the site of a major GULag camp. Variant: "What is the highest
building in Moscow? It is the building of the NKVD because from it you can see all of
Siberia." HPSSS, no. 128, schedule A, vol. 10, 30.

—Так ты же не верблюд?

—Ну да…. Поймают—кастрируют, а потом доказывай, что ты—не верблюд.

castrating camels.

—So what? You're not a camel.

—Yeah, but they'll catch you, castrate you, and then go ahead and prove all you want that you're not a camel.[10]

Один мелкий служащий ошибся этажом и пришёл на работу не в своё учреждение. Сел за стол и стал перебирать бумаги. Так он приходил три дня, пока начальник случайно не вскрыл «чужака». Допрос:

—Разве Вы на заметили, что работали не в своём учереждении?

—Замечал, что вроде как незнакомые лица кругом.

—А почему Вы не спросили?

—Побоялся….

A minor bureaucrat mixed up the floors in his building and went to the wrong office one morning. He sat down and got to work. He did this for three days until a supervisor accidentally discovered the "stranger." They asked him:

—Didn't you notice that you were working in the wrong institution?

—Well, it did seem to me that I was surrounded by unfamiliar faces.

—Why didn't you ask someone what was going on?

—I… was afraid to.

По требованию Всесоюзного Общества Советских Писателей в типовой авторский договор Госиздата был включён следующий пункт:

«Автор заранее признаёт ошибки в своём будущем произведении, отрекается от него и чистосердечно раскаивается в том, что написал эту возмутительную халтуру, искажающую советскую действительность и играющую на руку поджигателям войны».

At the request of the All-Union Society of Soviet Writers [sic, Soviet Writers' Union], the following line was added to the State Publishing House's standard book contract:

"The author admits in advance to the mistakes in his forthcoming work, denounces it, and sincerely regrets that he ever wrote such an appalling travesty that perverts Soviet reality and plays into the hands of warmongers."

Один НКВДист заметил, что какой-то человек, встречая его каждое утро на улице, снимает шапку и говорит:

An NKVD agent noticed that every morning, as he passed a particular fellow on the street, the guy would take off his

---

[10] For a variant, see Louis Fischer, ed., *Thirteen Who Fled* (New York: Harper, 1949), 190; Talmadge, "The Enjoyment of Laughter in Russia," 49–50; oblique reference to this joke is made in HPSSS, no. 387, schedule A, vol. 20, 41; no. 1664, schedule A, vol. 36, 15.

—Добрый вечер!

Однажды НКВДист остановил его:

—Кто Вы такой, и почему Вы говорите «добрый вечер», когда теперь утро?

—Я гражданин... я видите... как только встречаю Вас, так у меня в глазах темнеет....

hat and say "Good evening!" to him. Finally, the NKVD agent stopped him.

—Who are you and why are you saying "good evening" to me when it is actually morning?

—Uh, I'm nobody, really.... It's just that whenever I run into you, everything grows dark....[11]

У Сталина пропала трубка. Он позвонил в НКВД и приказал разыскать её. Через два часа сам нашёл её в своём собственном сапоге. Звонит опять в НКВД:

—Нэ надо, нашлась.

—Помилуйте, тов. Сталин, мы уже десять человек арестовали за Вашу трубку.

—Выпустить.

—Никак не возможно, все десять сознались.

Stalin's pipe went missing. He calls the NKVD and orders them to find it. Two hours later, he finds it himself in his own boot. He calls the NKVD again and says (in heavily accented Russian):

—Don't worry about it. I've found it.

—I'm sorry, Comrade Stalin, but we've already arrested ten people on account of your pipe!

—Let them go.

—But that's impossible sir. All ten have confessed.[12]

Раньше все ходили под богом, а теперь—под НКВД.

Before, everyone lived by the grace of God. Now, they live by the grace of the NKVD.[13]

В трамвае сидит какой-то гражданин с женой. Незнакомец, сидящий напротив, вздыхает:

—Ох, хо, хо, хо, хо!

Гражданин тихо, про себя:

—Эх, хе, хе, хе, хе !

Жена сердито:

A man and his wife are sitting in a trolley. A stranger sitting across from them sighs loudly:

—Ooooh!

The man also sighs quietly to himself:

—Ehhhh!

His wife angrily cuts him off:

---

[11] For a variant, see HPSSS, no. 147, schedule B, vol. 19, 30–31.

[12] For a variant, see HPSSS, no. 610, schedule B, vol. 20, 3. According to one Georgian party veteran, Stalin himself told a variant of this joke. See Akakii Mgeladze, *Stalin: Kakim ia ego znal—stranitsy nedavnego proshlogo* (Tbilisi: n.p., 2001), 168.

[13] For variants, see the entry from December 19, 1937 in "Diary of Stepan Filippovich Podlubny," in Veronique Garros, Natalia Korenevskaya, and Thomas Lahusen, eds., *Intimacy and Terror* (New York: New Press, 1995), 307; HPSSS, no. 1035, schedule A, vol. 31, 40.

—И сколько раз я тебе говорила: не разговаривай с незнакомыми про политику.

—How many times do I have to tell you not to talk about politics with strangers?[14]

☆ ☆ ☆

Один сталинский полицейский другому, указывая на одного гражданина:
—Интересно, о чём он сегодня молчит?

Pointing at a man on the street, one Stalinist policeman says to another:
—What do you s'pose that one's keeping quiet about today?

☆ ☆ ☆

Два гражданина потихоньку говорят про политику. Один «критикнул» власть, а другой испуганно:
—Ой, не говори такого.
—Почему?
—А может... кто-либо из нас двоих... сексот.

Two men are quietly talking to one-another about politics. One says something critical about the state and the other reacts in horror:
—Oh, don't say that!
—Why?
—One of us might be a... secret police agent!

☆ ☆ ☆

В СССР если встречаются двое, по крайней мере, один из них—сексот.

In the USSR, whenever two people get together, at least one of them is a secret police agent.[15]

☆ ☆ ☆

---

[14] Variant: "An elderly man, distressed with Soviet conditions, utters the mournful sigh 'oi!' on a tramcar. His wife hushes him and says, 'Fool, don't talk counter-revolution in public!" Lyons, *Moscow Carousel*, 323; also 339; HPSSS, no. 1492, schedule A, vol. 34, 21.

[15] Variant: "There is an anecdote that circulated in the Soviet Union in 1940 about the use of agents by the NKVD. A man wanted to put on a wedding for a daughter of his, but he was afraid that if he invited 20 or so people, they would be drinking and someone might say something, which would get everybody else in trouble and have the whole wedding branded as a counter-revolutionary meeting. So, the man [...] went to the NKVD and invited [them] to send someone to attend the wedding for security reason[s]. This request was refused. So, then he pulled from his pocket a list of the guests and he asked the NKVD to look over the list and to o.k. the people. [...T]he NKVD man looks at the list and says 'With the exception of one or two, they are all our people.'" HPSSS, no. 91, schedule A, vol. 7, 20; also no. 403, schedule B, vol. 20, 36; Lyons, *Moscow Carousel*, 338. This joke is narrated as an actual occurance in HPSSS, no. 1091, schedule A, vol. 31, 15.

В Советском Союзе каждый гражданин имеет два автомобиля: скорой помощи и «черный ворон».

In the USSR, every citizen has access to two cars: an ambulance and a "Black Raven."[16]

—Почему в этом году в СССР не было наводнений?

—Потому, что 180 миллионов советских граждан воды в рот набрали.

—Why was it so quiet in the USSR this year?

—Because 180 million Soviet citizens' lips were sealed.[17]

Население Советского Союза делится на три категории: на сидевших, сидящих и ожидающих сидеть.

The population of the Soviet Union can be divided into three categories: those who've done time, those who are doing time and those who expect to do time.

★ ★ ★

У каждого советского человека есть две тени: одна собственная, другая— НКВД.

Every Soviet citizen has two shadows: his own and the NKVD's.

★ ★ ★

Дальше едешь—тише будешь.

The further you go, the quieter you get.[18]

★ ★ ★

---

[16] NKVD vans used to transport suspects were called "Black Ravens" and "Black Marias." Variants include: "What do you mean, in the United States everybody has a car? In Soviet Russia everybody has two cars—the Black Maria and the ambulance." HPSSS, no. 30, schedule A, vol. 4, 35; also the diary entry from July 18, 1931, in Shitts, *Dnevnik "Velikogo pereloma,"* 316; TsGAIPD SPb f. 24, op. 2v, d. 1833, l. 34, cited in Davies, *Popular Opinion in Stalin's Russia*, 97.

[17] It is impossible to translate this joke literally—note the variant: "All the ice has thawed on the rivers and lakes and oceans so that there should be a lot of water, but there is not a drop of water. What happened to it? The answer is 170 millions of people took water into their mouth and keep quiet." HPSSS, no. 34, schedule A, vol. 4, 23.

[18] Mention of this joke in reference to Trotskii appears in a diary entry from January 5, 1925, in Bulgakov, *Dnevnik, Pis'ma, 1914–1940*, 87. Variants also include "The quieter you are, the further you'll go" (*Tishe edesh', dal'she budesh'*) in HPSSS, no. 61, schedule A, vol. 5, 13.

FIGURE 29. Karl Marx

«Бытиё определяет сознание». Эту формулу Маркса советские заключённые выговаривают так: «Битьё определяет сознание».

For Marx, being defines consciousness. Soviet prisoners expressed this maxim differently, however: "Beating defines consciousness."[19]

★ ★ ★

Про сталинские тюрьмы и лагеря советские заключённые говорят так: «Кто не был, тот будет; кто был, тот не забудет».

Inmates in the Stalinist camp system have a saying: "He who hasn't done time, will, and he who has done time, won't forget."[20]

★ ★ ★

—Где столица советской интеллигенции?
—Красноярск.

—What is the capital of the Soviet intelligentsia?
—Krasnoiarsk.[21]

★ ★ ★

В школе учитель замечает, что один мальчик ничего не делает, подходит к нему и говорит:
—Ты всё лодырничаешь, скажи-ка

A teacher notices a boy in school who isn't doing anything. He walks up to him and says:
—Hey, you're just loafing about. Tell

---

[19] For a variant, see Boikov, *Liudi sovetskoi tiur'my*, 357.

[20] The same joke is recounted in HPSSS, no. 305, schedule A, vol. 15, 24; Boikov, *Liudi sovetskoi tiur'my*, 359.

[21] One of the major hubs of the GULag.

мне, кто написал «Евгения Онегина».

—Не я, товарищ учитель, ей-богу не я...

—Что!!. Вот нахал! Вон из класса и пришли ко мне отца.

На следующее утро приходит отец. Учитель жалуется ему, что мальчишка — лентяй и на вопрос, кто написал «Евгения Онегина», нахально отвечает: «не я».

Отец примирительно:

—Товарищ учитель, а может и правда не он написал....

Учитель окончательно рассердился и вызывает мать мальчика. Та:

—Дорогой товарищ учитель, а может и правда не он написал такое.... А кроме того он же маленький....

Учитель рассверипел и выбежал из школы. На улице встречает знакомого священника.

—Так и так, отец Онуфрий, мальчишка ленится, спрашиваю, кто написал «Евгения Онегина», отвечает «не я». Вызываю отца, тот тоже считает, что сын не написал, мать — тоже. Чёрт знает, что такое....

—А скажите, будьте ласковы, ученик тот православный или иудей?

—Иудей, отец Онуфрий. Иудей.

—Ну, тогда «Евгения Онегина» написал он.

Учитель плюнул и побежал дальше. Встречает знакомого следователя НКВД и рассказывает ему всю историю.

—Любопытная история — задумчиво говорит следователь, — разберёмся....

Через неделю НКВДист снова встречает учителя:

—Ну вот, теперь всё выяснилось: Пришлось арестовать всех четверых — ученика, его отца, мать и священника.

me who wrote *Evgenii Onegin*?[22]

—Not me, Comrade Teacher, God knows, it wasn't me....

—What? Why, you rascal! Get out of my class this instant and send your father to me!"

The next day, his father comes in for a talk. The teacher complains to him that his boy is lazy and that he said "not me" when he was asked who wrote *Evgenii Onegin*.

The father replied in a conciliatory way:

—But Comrade Teacher, perhaps it's true that he didn't write it....

Furious, the teacher then summons the student's mother, who says:

—Dear Comrade Teacher, perhaps it's true that he didn't write it.... Besides, he's so young....

Fed up, the teacher storms out of the school. He runs into an acquaintance of his, a priest, on the street:

—Father Onufrii, listen to this: when I asked this lazy student of mine who wrote *Evgenii Onegin*, he replied "not me!" I called his father in and he said that his son didn't write it. I called the mother in and she said the same thing. What the hell is going on?"

—Ah-hem, tell me please, is the student Russian Orthodox or a Jew?

—A Jew, Father Onufrii, a Jew.

—Well, then, he must have been the one who wrote *Evgenii Onegin*.

So disgusted that he could just spit, the teacher kept walking and a few minutes later met an NKVD investigator he knew and told him the whole story.

—Hmm, how curious. We'll get to the bottom of this — said the investigator.

A week later, the teacher runs into his

---

[22] A. S. Pushkin's famous poem.

Вчера сознались стервы, что вчетвером написали «Евгения Онегина».

NKVD acquaintance again. The latter announces:

—You know, we just closed that case of yours. We arrested all four of them: the student, his father and mother, and the priest. Last night, the bastards finally confessed that they had all written *Evgenii Onegin* together.[23]

☆ ☆ ☆

На политзанятиях в полку политрук спрашивает солдат:

—Почему мы держим границу на замке?

Солдаты молчат.

—Ну, так как ребята? Почему же?

Один солдат:

—Чтоб люди из СССР не разбежались.

In a political studies course, a regimental political instructor asks his men:

—Why is the border kept under lock and key?

No one answers.

—Come on, guys, why?

One soldier replies:

—So that the people of the USSR will not run away?

☆ ☆ ☆

Ночью в квартиру стучит каблуками управдом и орёт:

—Пожар!... Горим!...

Перепуганный жилец, открывая дверь:

—Ну, слава Богу, а я уже думал худое....

Late one night, a superintendent bangs on an apartment door and then shouts:

—Fire! The building's on fire!

A frightened resident opens the door with relief:

—Oh, thank God. I was sure it was something worse....[24]

---

[23] For a variant, see HPSSS, no. 64, schedule A, vol. 6, 67–68. According to Stalin's daughter, the general secretary himself told a variant of this joke. See Svetlana Allilueva, *Only One Year*, trans. Paul Chavchavadze (New York: Harper and Row, 1969), 386.

[24] Variant: "At four o'clock in the morning there was a knock on the door of a Moscow house, which was occupied by five families. All of them leapt out of bed but none of them dared to open the door. The knocking grew louder. Finally, one of the tenants, Abram Abramovich, took his courage in both hands and finally opened the front door. He was heard whispering for a few moments with a man standing outside. Then he came back to his terrified fellow tenants with a bright smile on his face: 'Nothing to worry about, comrades—the house is on fire, that's all.'" Wolfgang Leonard, *Child of the Revolution*, trans. C. M. Woodhouse (Chicago: H. Regenry Co., 1967), 51; also Boikov, *Liudi sovetskoi tiur'my*, 365; Sokolova, "Iz starykh tetradei, 1935–1937," 360–61.

В одном из лагерей ГУЛАГа лекпом поставил такой диагноз смерти заключённого: «умер от дрэнологии».

Under "cause of death," a GULag orderly wrote in the file of a deceased inmate: "blackjackitis."[25]

В камере смертников комиссия спрашивает про последнее желание. Один осуждённый:
—Я хотел бы поесть малинки.
—Так сейчас же зима!
—Ничего, я подожду.
—А может Вы чего иного пожелали бы?
—Иного? Хорошо. Прошу похоронить меня рядом со Сталиным.
—Так он же ещё жив!
—Ничего, я подожду.

A death row commission asks a prisoner if he has any last wishes. He answers:
—I'd like to have some raspberries.
—But it's winter!
—That's okay. I'll wait.
—Maybe there's something else you'd like?
—Something else? Okay, I'd like to be buried next to Stalin.
—But he is still alive!
—That's alright. I'll wait.[26]

✯ ✯ ✯

Армянина осудили на десять лет в Соловки. Судья спрашивает его, что он имеет сказать.
—Какая власть на Соловках?
—Советская.
—Тогда гоните дальше.

An Armenian is to be sent to the far north to Solovki for ten years. The judge asks him if he has any questions about his sentence.
—Who runs Solovki?
—The Soviets.
—Then send me further, please.[27]

✯ ✯ ✯

—Вы слыхали, что Петрова расстреляли?
—Тише Вы, смотрите он сам идёт по той стороне улицы.
—Так он сам ещё не знает.

—Have you heard that Petrov's been shot?
—Shhh! Isn't that Petrov himself walking on the other side of the street?
—Yeah, he hasn't heard yet.

---

[25] From "blackjack" (*dren*), a police baton used to beat prisoners.

[26] Variant: "A certain political person was judged to be guilty and sentenced to death. After the sentence, he was asked to tell his last wish before he died. He replied 'Yes, I have such a wish.' He was asked what it was […] 'After my death, I should like to be buried next to Stalin.' 'But,' he was told, 'Stalin is still alive.' He replied, 'Yes, I know, but I can wait for him to die, I'm not in a hurry.'" HPSSS, no. 98, schedule A, vol. 7, 14; also *Sovetskie anekdoty*, 40–41; *Dlia nekuriashchikh*, 149–50; Lyons, *Moscow Carousel*, 328.

[27] For a variant, see HPSSS, no. 1486, schedule A, vol. 34, 23.

У приговорённого к расстрелу армянина спрашивают его последнее желание.

—Хочу вступить в партию.

—Зачем Вам это? Вас же расстреляют!

—Вот именно! Одной сволочью меньше будет!

An Armenian who is sentenced to be shot is asked if he has any final requests.

—I'd like to join the party.

—Why? You're going to be shot!

—I know. But then there'll be one fewer of you bastards.[28]

★ ★ ★

—Вы слышали? Сарагосу взяли!

—Что?! С семьёй?

—Какое! Это—город.

—Что?! Уже целыми городами стали брать!!!

—Have you heard? They've taken Saragossa!

—What? With her family?

—Huh? Saragossa is a city!

—What? They've begun arresting entire cities?[29]

---

[28] For variants, see Lyons, *Moscow Carousel*, 327; *Sovetskie anekdoty*, 40–41.

[29] A city in north central Spain captured by republican forces in the fall of 1937 during the Spanish Civil War. For a variant, see Sokolova, "Iz starykh tetradei, 1935–1937," 364; another, from well before the conflict in Spain, is printed in *Sovetskie anekdoty*, 30.

Storm Clouds Gather

Although the Great Terror receded toward the end of 1938, Soviet society received little respite. World events led many to believe that the long-predicted showdown with capitalist forces abroad was imminent. A proxy war in Spain against Nazi Germany and Fascist Italy dominated headlines amid reports of more sporadic clashes with the Japanese in the far east. At home, the release of blockbuster films about Peter the Great, Aleksandr Nevskii, and other historic Russian heroes suggested that Soviet propaganda was shifting from proletarian internationalism to something more reminiscent of Russian nationalism.[1] Mobilization was the order of the day and shrill patriotic rhetoric in the press was accompanied by new legislation which attempted to enforce labor discipline in the workplace. Perhaps the greatest shock, however, was the signing of the August 1939 Molotov-Ribbentrop treaty after years of propaganda revolving around the malevolence of the Nazi regime.

Such reversals, combined with a series of unconvincing "wars of liberation" between 1939 and 1940 in eastern Poland, Finland, and the Baltic states, were greeted with disbelief and cynicism by jokesters in Soviet society. Although few had reason to distrust *Pravda*'s description of the threats that the society faced, the inscrutability of the official line gave rise to uncertainty, confusion, and popular dissembling.

В 1939 году театр в Москве готовился к возобновлению оперы Глинки «Жизнь за царя», переименованной в «Ивана Сусанина». В последнем акте оперы имеется сцена со звоном в церковные колокола. Звонаря, в театре, конечно, не нашлось. Поиски по Москве не дали

In 1939, a Moscow theater began the rehabilitation of Glinka's opera *A Life for the Tsar* under the title *Ivan Susanin*.[2] In the final act of the opera, a scene required the peal of church bells and of course no one in the theater knew how to ring a bell. A search throughout

---

[1] On this ideological about-face, see David Brandenberger, *National Bolshevism: Stalinist Mass Culture and the Formation of Modern Russian National Identity, 1931–1956* (Cambridge, MA: Harvard University Press, 2002), chaps. 2–3.

[2] M. I. Glinka's opera revolved around popular resistance to Polish invaders during Muscovy's early seventeenth-century interregnum. It was revived six months before the signing of the Molotov-Ribbentrop treaty in order to prepare Soviet public opinion for hostilities with Poland.

результатов: бывшие церковные звонари давно переменили профессию и теперь не рисковали заикнуться о своём прошлом.

Кто-то из артистов нашёлся:

—Пусть директор обратится в НКВД. У них, наверно, звонарь найдётся....

Через час после телефонной просьбы директора «Чёрный ворон» доставил в театр опытнейшего церковного звонаря. Хорошо звонил... под охраной.

Moscow also yielded no results—all bell ringers had long ago switched professions and were not about to admit to their former occupations. Finally, one of the actors had an idea:

—The director should ask the NKVD. If anyone can find us a ringer, it's the NKVD....

An hour after the director placed a call to the NKVD, a "Black Raven" drove up with an experienced bell ringer. And he did a good job... despite the leg irons.

Как известно, всенародная перепись в СССР в 1937 году была осуждена «любимым вождём» как «вредительская». Не те, кто нужно, переписывали, не так, как нужно, подсчитывали. Новая перепись в 1939 году дала «правильные» результаты. Весь комсомол был мобилизован на проведение этого «великого общегосударственного дела».

Два комсомольца, производящие перепись, обходят квартиры. Заходят в комнату к одной девушке. Один спрашивает, второй заполняет карточку. Первый:

—Ваше имя, отчество, фамилия? Сколько лет?

Девушка отвечает.

—Профессия?

—Педикюрша.

—Что?

—Педикюрша

—Чаво?!

—Пе-ди-кюр-ша!

Оба комсомольца в недоумении. Второй:

—Вань, что это такое? Как писать?

As is well known, the 1937 all-union census was condemned by the "beloved leader" as "sabotage." People were counted who shouldn't have been and others weren't counted who should have been. A new census in 1939 produced more "correct" results. The entire Komsomol was mobilized in order to conduct this "great event of public interest."

Two Komsomol members, collecting information for the census, went from apartment to apartment. When they got to one young woman's room, they proceeded as usual, the first asking her the questions and the second writing down her answers. The first one asks:

—First name? Patronymic? Last name? Age?

She tells them.

—Your profession?

—Pedicurist.

—Huh?

—Pedicurist.

—Huh?

—Ped-i-cur-ist!

The Komsomol members are dumbfounded. The second asks the first:

—Пиши просто: б….

—Van'ia, what's that? How do I spell it?

—I dunno. Just write "w-h-o-r-e."

★ ★ ★

Группа советских командированных возвращалась с Запада в СССР. Везли они Калинину, по его просьбе, бутылку французского коньяка наивысшего качества. Но длинна и скучна дорога через Польшу; все напитки выпиты, а жажда мучила невыносимо. Ребята решили выпить и калининскую бутылочку, а в Москве налить чего-нибудь попроще и вручить Михаилу Ивановичу.

Так и сделали. В Москве купили дрянного советского коньячку, вылили во французскую бутылку, аккуратно натянули фирменный колпачок и явились на приём к Калинину.

—Не знаем, Михаил Иванович, понравится ли Вам. Прогнил капитализм совсем—даже коньяк во Франции испортился….

Калинин попробовал, протянул «да-а…» и впервые уверовал в гнилость Запада.

A group of Soviet officials were returning by train to the USSR from a trip abroad. At Kalinin's request, they were bringing a bottle of the finest French cognac with them. But the trip through Poland was long and boring and once the officials had drunk everything else, their thirst grew unbearable. The guys decided to drink Kalinin's cognac and then fill the bottle with something else in Moscow before giving it to him.

And that's just what they proceeded to do. In Moscow, they bought a bottle of lousy Soviet cognac, poured it into the French bottle, screwed the cap back on carefully and went to meet with Kalinin.

—We're not sure if you'll like it, Mikhail Ivanovich. Capitalism is in its final stage of decay and even French cognac has gone downhill….

Kalinin tried it, sighed, and believed for the first time in his life that the West actually was rotten after all.

★ ★ ★

—Кто лучшая доярка Советского Союза?

—Адольф Гитлер.

—Who's the best milkmaid in the USSR?

—Adolf Hitler.[3]

★ ★ ★

—Какая разница между коммунизмом и фашизмом?

—Почти никакой. Если и есть расхождения, то только по двум вопросам: по транспортному и

—What's the difference between communism and fascism?

—Almost nothing. If there is a difference, it concerns two issues associated with transportation and land

---

[3] Under the terms of the 1939 Molotov-Ribbentrop treaty, the USSR supplied Hitler with subsidized grain, oil, timber, and other raw materials and agricultural goods.

земельному.

—Какие же?

—Фашисты хотят ездить на коммунистах, а те—на фашистах. Опять же фашисты хотят коммунистов угробить, а коммунисты— фашистов.

use.

—What are they?

—The fascists want a free ride on the backs of the communists while the communists want to ride on the fascists' backs. Similarly, the fascists want to bury the communists and the communists want to bury the fascists.[4]

Когда Сталин, совместно с Гитлером, «освободил Польшу» в сентябре 1939 года, советская пропаганда трещала: «протянем руку помощи нашим братьям».

Знакомый с этой «рукой» подсоветский народ говорил:

— «Мы протянем им руку, а ноги они сами протянут».

When Stalin "liberated" Poland along with Hitler in September 1939, Soviet propagandists announced over and over: "Let's give our brothers a helping hand."

The Soviet people, well-acquainted with this "hand," said:

—We'll give 'em a hand and they'll give up the ghost.[5]

Командированный из Москвы в Териоки еврей вдруг узнаёт в рядах «финской народной армии» своего хорошего знакомого:

—Хайм, а как вы сюда попали?!

—Я не Хайм, я—финн.

—Что?! Ну, это Вы бросьте, Вы же из Минска.

—Пошел вон!

—Удивительно…. Я слыхал, что бывают финские мины, но чтобы минские финны?! …. Слышу в первый раз.

A Jew from Moscow serving in Terijoki[6] during the Soviet-Finnish War suddenly recognizes a friend of his within the ranks of the so-called "Finnish People's Army."

—Khaim, how did you get here?

—I'm not Khaim… I'm a Finn.

—What? Aw, come on. You're a Jew from Minsk.

—Shut up!

—Amazing… I've heard of Finnish mines, but never Finnish Khaims….[7]

---

[4] See an earlier variant of this joke on page 47.

[5] Variant: "The joke was that Molotov extends the friendly hand of unity, and the Baltics extend their feet (i.e., die)." HPSSS, no. 1240, schedule A, vol. 32, 48.

[6] Headquarters of the ostensibly indigenous Soviet Karelian war effort during the Winter War.

[7] For variants, see S. Dmitriev, *Party and Political Organs of the Soviet Army*, no. 36, *Research Program on the USSR Mimeograph Series* (New York: Research Program on the USSR, 1953), 20; HPSSS, no. 135, schedule B, vol. 7, 13.

FIGURE 30. V. M. Molotov

В «освобождённые от капиталистического ига» Польшу и Прибалтику Сталин посылал спички, соль и «носителей советской культуры»: партработников, полицейских, артистов и писателей. Поделившись своей «культурой» с освобождёнными братьями, они захватывали побольше туфель и мануфактуры и возвращались на «любимую родину».

Вернувшись из Польши, Лебедев-Кумач явился к Молотову. Тот оглядел его с головы до ног и сказал:

—Ты, брат, из Лебедева-Кумача в Лебедева-Коверкота превратился!

After "liberating" Poland and the Baltic states from the "capitalist yoke," Stalin sent matches, salt and "representatives of Soviet culture"—party officials, policemen, artists, and writers—to the region. After sharing their "culture" with their newly-liberated brethren, they snatched up lots of shoes and clothing before returning to their "beloved motherland."

Lebedev-Kumach[8] was summoned to see Molotov after he returned from Poland. The latter looked him over from head to toe and said:

—You, my brother, have turned from Lebedev-Kumach into Lebedev-Debauch.

В те времена НКВД распространял разные слухи и сплетни для дезинформации подсоветского населения. Основной мотив был: «Польша отсталая, и мы несём туда культуру». Ходил такой анекдот о советской бесплатной медпомощи:

During these years, the NKVD spread rumors, gossip and disinformation in Soviet society. The main motif was: "Poland is backward and we're bringing them culture." The following joke soon appeared regarding free health care in the newly-Sovietized part of Poland:

---

[8] V. I. Lebedev-Kumach (1898–1949), Soviet lyricist credited with popular songs from films like *The Happy-Go-Lucky Guys*, *Circus*, and *Volga-Volga*.

В амбулатории советский врач принимает больных. Входит рослая пышная девка. Врач заполняет карточку:

—Имя? Фамилия? На что жалуешься?

Девка отвечает.

Врач:

—Ну, ладно, иди за ширму, раздевайся, сейчас посмотрим.

Врач продолжает писать. Через минуту идёт за ширму. Девка стоит там в нерешительности. Врач:

—Чего же ты не раздеваешься? Я же сказал тебе!

Врач возвращается к столику, пишет дальше. Через минуту идёт снова за ширму. Девка продолжает стоять неподвижно. Врач:

—Ну, чего же ты не раздеваешься?

—А ты сам, чорт, чего не раздеваешься?!

A Soviet doctor is seeing patients in a clinic. A plump young woman comes into his office and he begins filling out her chart:

—First name? Last name? What seems to be bothering you?

The woman tells him.

The doctor then says:

—Okay. Why don't you go behind the curtain and take your clothes off.

The doctor continues writing for a moment and then draws back the curtain, only to find the woman standing there hesitantly.

—Why haven't you gotten undressed? I asked you to get undressed.

The doctor returns to his desk and writes a bit more. A minute later, he draws the curtain back and the woman is still standing there, unmoving. He asks:

—So why haven't you taken your clothes off?

—Speak for yourself, jerk. When are you going to take yours off?

Анекдот, распространявшийся советской пропагандой во время войны с Финляндией:

Финны запросили шведов о помощи танками. Шведы переспросили телеграммой:

—Прислать вам один танк или все три?

A joke spread by Soviet propagandists during the Winter War with Finland went as follows:

The Finns ask the Swedes to loan them some tanks. The Swedes send a telegram back:

—How many tanks should we send? Just one or all three?[9]

---

[9] In spite of Andreevich's allegations, there is no evidence that Soviet propagandists disseminated jokes as part of their official duties.

FIGURE 31. Baku oil fields

На торжественном заседании в Баку по поводу 20-летия Азербайджанской ССР Калинин распространялся о всех благодеяниях, оказанных Москвой Азербайджану, а также о «самосто-ятельности Азербайджана». С ответным словом благодарности выступил старый азербайджанец, который на ломаном русском языке сказал:

Спасыба, савецка власт, болшой спасыба:

Аз наш—земля ваш, ай спасыба,
Аз наш—хлеб ваш, ай спасыба,
Аз наш—рыба ваш, ай спасыба;
Аз наш—нэфт ваш, ай спасыба!

At a Baku celebration in honor of the 20th anniversary of the founding of Soviet Azerbaidzhan,[10] Kalinin spoke at length about all the assistance Moscow had rendered Azerbaidzhan, as well as about the republic's new "indepen-dence." An old Azeri man then stood up to give words of thanks in broken Russian:

Thank you, Soviet power, thank you!
Our land is now your land, thank you very much!
Our bread is now your bread, thank you very much!
Our fish is now your fish, thank you very much!
Our oil is now your oil, thank you very much![11]

---

[10] The Azeri Soviet Socialist Republic was founded April 28, 1920.

[11] For a variant, see "Sovetskie anekdoty," 54.

В трамвае в 8 ч.10 м. утра разбили стекло. Кондуктор, обращаясь к пассажирам:

—Граждане, кто разбил стекло?

Полвагона отвечает:

—Я, я, я, я, я....

A window is broken in a tram at 8:10 a.m. The conductor turns to the passengers:

—Citizens, who broke this window?

Half of the car answers:

—I did. No, I did. I did. No, it was me....[12]

☆ ☆ ☆

Женщина вскакивает в трамвай с панталонами под мышкой.

—Где дают? Где купила?

—Купила!? Дома надеть не успела!

A woman jumps onto a tram with a pair of panties tucked under her arm. People ask her:

—Were those for sale? Where did you buy them?

—Buy them? I just didn't have time to put them on this morning![13]

☆ ☆ ☆

В суде:

—Подсудимый, сколько Вам лет?

—35.

—Как 35? По документам Вам 45!

—Оно то так, но последние 10 лет я жил в колхозе, а разве это жизнь?

In court:

—Accused, how old are you?

—35.

—What do you mean, 35? According to your documents, you're 45!

—That's true, but I've been on a collective farm for the past ten years. Can that really be considered living?[14]

---

[12] In order to reinforce discipline in the workplace, the Soviet government criminalized absenteeism and tardiness by official decree on June 26, 1940. Here, commuters seek a police ticket for the infraction in order to account for their lateness to work. Reference is made to this practice in HPSSS, no. 9, schedule A, vol. 1, 85; no. 49, schedule A, vol. 5, 11; no. 1313, schedule A, vol. 33, 98.

[13] Variant: "a woman was running one morning with her panties in her hand. Panties and such unmentionables were particularly hard to find as a result of the government's lack of concern for anything not pertaining to heavy industry. This woman was thus shortly stopped by a great many people desirous of purchasing these panties which she was, they assumed, holding openly for sale. 'These are not for sale. I did not have time to put them on in fear of arriving late for work,' she managed to say while continuing to run." HPSSS, no. 1296, schedule A, vol. 33, 19; also no. 49, schedule A, vol. 5, 11; no. 1706, schedule A, vol. 37, 47.

[14] A satirical reference to a worker's boast at a 1935 Stakhanovite congress: "Comrades, I am forty-five years old, but I feel like I've been alive for only eighteen years." See *Geroini sotsialisticheskogo truda* (Moscow: Partizdat, 1936), 25. A variant: "A Soviet citizen was brought before the NKVD for questioning. When he was asked 'How old are you?' he replied, 'Fifty years.' The official replied, 'Please, show me your documents.' The man gave them to him. The official, after looking through the documents

✯ ✯ ✯

Однажды продавцы в госмагазинах получили особо строгий приказ отвечать покупателям только вежливо. В мануфактурный магазин заходит привередливая дамочка. Просит показать товар. Не нравится. Спрашивает еще. Опять бракует. Перебрала почти весь товар и спрашивает ещё.

Продавец, наклонившись, шипит:

—Гражданочка, станьте, пожалуйста, на моё место, а я пойду к чёртовой матери.

Once upon a time, strict orders were given to the sales assistants in state stores to be scrupulously polite with their customers. One day, a pedantic woman comes into a fabric store. She asks to see a piece of merchandise, but doesn't like it. After asking to see another, she rejects it as well. Having rejected most of the goods in the store, she asks to see still more.

Finally, the sales assistant hisses:

—My dear citizenness, let's switch places for a moment. You come over here and take my place and I will go burn in hell.

✯ ✯ ✯

В трамвае кто-то громко чихнул. Милиционер обращается к публике:

—Кто чихнул, граждане?

Все умолкли. Милиционер настойчиво:

—Граждане! Кто чихнул?

Все замерли, боятся смотреть друг на друга. Милиционер в третий раз:

—Граждане! Я вас спрашиваю, кто чихнул?

В углу слышен шёпот:

—Бабуся, милая, ты старая, тебе уже нечего бояться, скажи, что ты.

Старуха слабым голосом:

—Я, родименький, по старости чихнула....

Someone sneezes loudly in a tram. A police officer asks:

—Who sneezed, citizens?

Everyone is silent. The police officer again asks:

—Citizens, who sneezed?

Everyone freezes, afraid to look at one another. The police officer asks for the third time:

—Citizens, I'll ask you once more: who sneezed?

Someone whispers at the back of the tram:

—Granny, dear, you're old and you don't have anything to lose. Say that it was you.

The old lady speaks up with a weak voice:

—Sonny, it was me. I sneezed from old age.

---

said, 'But you are really 70 years of age. How do you explain the fact that your documents say that you are 70 and you told me that you are 50?' The man replied, 'The first 50 years I lived before the revolution. The last 20 years I have spent under Communism. I do not consider that during this period I lived.'" HPSSS, no. 98, schedule A, vol. 7, 14.

FIGURE 32. Soviet border guard

Милиционер протискивается до старушки и лихо берет под козырёк:
—Будьте здоровы, бабушка!

The police officer pushes his way through the crowd up to the old lady, touches the brim of his cap, and says:
— Gesundheit, granny![15]

Еврей удирает заграницу. Чувствует, что его заметил пограничник. Еврей поспешно спускает штаны и садится на собачий «след»:
—Ты что здесь делаешь?
Еврей, показывая на «след».
—Не видишь, что ли?
—Так это же собачье!

A Jew is sneaking across the border and realizes that he's been spotted by a border guard. He quickly drops his pants and crouches over some dog droppings.
—What are you doing here?
The Jew points to the droppings.
—Can't you see?
—But those look like they're from a

[15] A campaign on the eve of the war encouraged the militia to treat Soviet citizens with greater respect and better manners. Variants of this joke include: "There were numerous impositions upon the rights of the workers. Later, the government realised that this strictness led to wide dissatisfaction. So, a new *ukaz* [decree] was issued which ordered policemen to be more polite to people. For example, once a streetcar was passing a policeman and he heard a loud sneeze. The policeman promptly stopped the streetcar and demanded to know who sneezed. The passengers were frightened because not many knew of the new *ukaz*. Finally, a lady admitted that she had sneezed. The policeman tipped his hat and said: 'Good health to you' and walked away." HPSSS, no. 1467, schedule A, vol. 34, 10–11.

—А жизнь у нас человеческая, что ли?

dog!

—If you treat us like dogs, what do you expect?

★ ★ ★

Два еврея переходили границу, натянув на себя шкуру коровы и ступая как-бы четырьмя ногами.

Вдруг передний еврей дико вопит:

—Соломон, мы пропали!

—Что? Пограничник?

—Нет, хуже, бык!

Two Jews were sneaking across the border under a cow's hide, doing their best to walk like the four-legged beast. Suddenly, the Jew in the front cries out:

—Solomon, we're screwed!

—What do you mean? A border guard?

—No, worse—a bull.

★ ★ ★

Сталину приснился Ленин. Подходит к нему и спрашивает:

—Ну, как дела?

—Хараши: кончил коллективизацию.

—А народ?

—Всэ са мной.

—А дальше?

—Всэ, как адын, са мной!

—Здорово! А что дальше будет?

—Камунызм!

—Славно! А народ?

—Канэшно, всэ будут со мной!

Ленин, подумав:

—Да... думаю, что к тому времени они все будут... со мной.

Stalin had a dream about Lenin, who came up to him and asked:

—So, how are things going?

Stalin replies (in heavily accented Russian):

—Fine. I've finished collectivization.

—And the people?

—They're with me.

—And in the future?

—They'll be with me, down to the last man!

—Great. What's to come?

—Communism.

—Terrific. And the people?

—They'll be with me, of course!

Lenin thinks to himself for a moment and says:

—Hmm... by that time, I suspect that they'll actually all be right here with me.[16]

★ ★ ★

У грузина, бежавшего заграницу, спрашивают:

—Ну, как, жить можно в СССР?

—Жив будышь, только будышь худой, худой.

A Georgian who escaped across the border is asked:

—So, is it possible to live in the USSR?

—Yes, you can live, but you'll be thin-thin-thin.

---

[16] For a variant, see Lyons, *Moscow Carousel*, 337.

FIGURE 33. Kalinin presenting champion beet-picker
Maria Demchenko with a medal

В приёмной Калинина была
получена телеграмма:

—Заготовьте ордена. Я и Абрамович
бежим из Харькова в Москву на
цыпочках.

Секретарь Калинина сердито
буркнул:

—Чёрта вам! Ордена получат двое,
которые из Минска ползут сюда на
четвереньках.

A telegram arrives in Kalinin's
chancellery:

—Get some medals ready. Abramovich
and I are running from Khar'kov to
Moscow on our tiptoes.

Kalinin's secretary scoffs:

—Who the hell cares! Our medals are
reserved for the next two guys who do
the commando crawl from Minsk on all
fours![17]

---

[17] On the eve of the war, Soviet mass culture focused considerable attention on popular athletics, physical fitness, and aviation. Cynics, according to Andreevich, felt this
was a way of preparing potential draftees for military service. See *Kreml' i narod*, 76.

The Great Patriotic War

Although by 1941 the USSR had spent over a decade preparing for war, the Nazis' launch of Operation Barbarossa on June 22 of that year caught the society unawares. Stalin had suspected that rumors of imminent attack were the work of Nazi counterintelligence and was determined not to succumb to provocation.[1] This explains his instructions to *Pravda* to quash rumors of new tensions in the Nazi-Soviet relationship in the days and weeks before the invasion. It also clarifies why Stalin attempted to rein in the Red Army even after the first bombs began to fall, still convinced that the invasion was nothing more than aggressive saber-rattling.

In the wake of this surprise attack, a surge of genuinely patriotic emotion swept through Soviet society, discouraging the appearance of even gallows humor related to the war. Although defeatist rumors began to appear during the fall of 1941,[2] jokesters generally seem to have respected social and political taboos that warned against commentary that could be understood as demoralizing or disloyal. Ultimately, most of the humor that circulated between 1941 and 1945 was quite tame in comparison with the jokes of the interwar period, barbs being restricted to innocuous targets such as the command staff's loss of initiative and the poor quality of military hardware.

Perhaps the only real wartime innovation in Stalin-era political humor was the emergence of a cycle of anti-Semitic jokes deriding Jews for their reluctance to risk life and limb in defense of the USSR. Precipitated by the Soviet news media's emphasis on "Russianness" and its underreporting of Jewish contributions to the war effort, these jokes explained the apparent absence of Jewish heroism by alleging that draft-age Jews were sitting out the war in Central Asian evacuation. Fueled by the war's atmosphere of austerity and suffering, everyday chauvinism combined with epithets such as "Tashkent partisan" to give rise to widespread anti-Semitic sentiments that would persist deep into the 1940s.[3]

---

[1] *Sekrety Gitlera na stole u Stalina—razvedka i kontrrazvedka o podgotovke germanskoi agressii protiv SSSR, mart–iiun' 1941 g.: Dokumenty iz Tsentral'nogo arkhiva FSB* (Moscow: Mosgorarkhiv, 1995), 10–11.

[2] Tsentral'nyi arkhiv FSB, published in *Moskva voennaia, 1941-1945: Memuary i arkhivnye dokumenty* (Moscow: Mosgorarkhiv, 1995), 49–50; RGASPI f. 17, op. 125, d. 85, l. 79; HPSSS, no. 13, schedule A, vol. 2, 42.

[3] Brandenberger, *National Bolshevism: Stalinist Mass Culture and the Formation of Modern Russian National Identity*, 179–80; see also Amir Weiner's discussion of the "Tashkent

В 1941 году на фронте:
—В чём сходство между немецкими самолётами и советскими?
—И те и другие летают над советскими тылами.

At the front in 1941:
—What do German and Soviet airplanes have in common?
—Both fly in Soviet airspace.

Частушка, которую солдаты сочинили и распевали на фронте:
Жил на свете грозный Ил,
На штурмовку он ходил.
Снизу у него броня,
Остальное всё—........!

A couplet composed and sung at the front:
Once upon a time there was the fearsome IL,[4]
A fighter and tank buster—quite the deal.
It had armor underneath in case it was hit,
Other than that, though, it was a piece of shit.

Сталин лично инструктирует лётчиков, которые должны бомбить Берлин:
—Здэсь—указывает на карте,—военные заводы. Унычтожить! Здэсь—казармы—унычтожить! Здэсь... Министерство Пропаганды. Того из вас, кто сбросит хоть одну бомбу, расстреляю!

. Stalin personally instructed the first wave of Soviet pilots to bomb Berlin.[5] Pointing to a map, he said (in heavily accented Russian):
—Here are the military factories. Destroy them! Here are the barracks. Destroy them! Here is the Ministry of Propaganda. If you hit it with even a single bomb, I'll have you shot![6]

---

partisan" genre of popular anti-Semitism in *Making Sense of War: The Second World War and the Fate of the Bolshevik Revolution* (Princeton, NJ: Princeton University Press, 2001), 114–22, 191–235, 271–97, 375–77.

[4] A reference to the IL-2 "Shturmovik," an all-purpose fighter produced by the Iliushin aircraft design team.

[5] The Soviet air force's first bombing run over Berlin took place on August 8, 1941.

[6] The racist screed promoted by Nazi Minister of Propaganda Joseph Goebbels often served Soviet interests as readily as it did the German cause. Another joke satirizing Axis ideology focused on fascist Italy: "Mussolini's son asked him once at breakfast: 'Daddy, what is national socialism?' Mussolini answered: 'Esh' i molchi [Shut up and eat],' the principle of national socialism." HPSSS, no. 335, schedule A, vol. 17, 51.

На призывном пункте медицинская комиссия опрашивает призываемых.

Один жалуется:

—У меня лёгкие больные.

—Ничего, вон у Андреева, члена Политбюро, также лёгкие больные, а он служит советской власти.

Следующий жалуется:

—У меня сердце больное.

—У Ворошилова также, а он служит Красной Армии.

Доходит очередь до еврея, который всё время внимательно прислушивался:

—Я идиот.

—Ничего, Калинин вон круглый идиот, а служит советской власти….

At a draft office, a medical commission is looking over the draftees.

One complains:

—I have weak lungs.

—That's okay. Andreev,[7] a Politburo member, also has weak lungs and he serves Soviet power.

The next complains:

—I have a weak heart.

—So does Voroshilov, and he serves in the Red Army.

They work through the line of draftees until they reach a Jew who had been listening carefully.

—I'm a fool.

—That's okay. Kalinin is a total moron and still serves Soviet power.

☆ ☆ ☆

На военный корабль прибывает пополнение из моряков запаса. Офицер, принимая пополнение, спрашивает каждого прибывшего о его морской специальности. Доходит очередь до еврея. Офицер спрашивает:

—Вы боцман?

—Нет.

—Лоцман?

—Нет.

—А кто же Вы?

—Я?! Кацман.

Reinforcements are sent to a naval vessel. The officer who receives the men asks each one what he had been trained to do. The line wound down to a Jew. The officer asks:

—Boatman?

—No.

—Gunman?

—No.

—Who the hell are you?

—Me? Katsman!

☆ ☆ ☆

На фронте комиссар орёт: « За советскую родину!», «За любимого Сталина!», и солдаты бросаются в атаку. Только один солдат—еврей— спрятался в кусты.

После атаки командир разыскал его и стал ругать: подлец, мерзавец, трус!

Еврей (про себя):

At the front, a commissar yells "For the Soviet Motherland!" "For Our Beloved Stalin!" and his soldiers charge into battle. All except for one soldier, a Jew, who hides in the bushes.

After the attack, the commander tracks him down and scolds him: bastard, scum, coward!

The Jew mutters to himself:

---

[7] A. A. Andreev (1895–1971), a party hierarch.

—Лучше быть пять минут трусом, чем всю жизнь мертвецом.

—It's better to be a coward for five minutes than a corpse for the rest of my life.[8]

Во время войны к советскому генералу, командовавшему дивизией на фронте, поступает донесение: «немцы взяли в плен «Военторг». Генерал злорадно:

—Так им и надо. Я с ним 20 лет мучился, пусть теперь фрицы попробуют!

During the war, a Soviet general commanding a division at the front learns from a report that the Germans have seized a military department store.

—Just what they deserve. I've suffered on account of that store for 20 years. Let the Fritzes have a try!

На ялтинской конференции:

После одного из трудных совещаний Рузвельт, Черчилль и Сталин поехали кататься по парку. Поперёк узкого мостика через речку лежал бык и преграждал дорогу.

Рузвельт крикнул на быка—тот ухом не повёл. Тыкнул его палкой—бык не обратил внимания.

Подошёл Черчилль и крепко пнул быка ногой. Не подействовало.

Тогда подошёл Сталин, наклонился к быку и шепнул ему что-то на ухо. Бык вскочил, дико заревел и убежал.

Сталин не открыл своим партнёрам, что именно он сказал быку. Но шофёр Сталина, подслушавший слова «хозяина», разъяснил:

At the Yalta conference:

After one of their most difficult sessions, Roosevelt, Churchill, and Stalin went for a drive on the estate grounds. Suddenly, they noticed a bull lying on the ground in front of a narrow bridge, blocking the road.

Roosevelt shouted at the bull but he didn't bat an eye. He poked him with his cane, but the bull didn't pay any attention.

Churchill walked up to him and gave him a swift kick with his foot. It had no effect.

Then Stalin walked up to the bull, leaned over him and whispered something into his ear. The bull jumped to its feet, bellowed loudly and ran off.

Stalin never revealed to his colleagues what he had whispered to the bull, but his chauffeur heard what the boss said and explained later:

---

[8] Many wartime jokes questioned Jewish commitment to the Soviet cause, e.g.: "Far in the rear, two Jews walk up to a map at a train station and say: 'So, what have we retaken today?'" Another: "A Jewish evacuee's telegram: 'I've made it to Novosibirsk successfully. If the Motherland demands it, I am prepared to go even further.'" See the diary entry from January 17, 1944, in A. N. Boldyrev, *Osadnaia zapis': Blokadnyi dnevnik* (St. Petersburg: Evropeiskii dom/Evropeiskii universitet, 1998), 319.

—Сталин сказал быку: «отдам в колхоз».

—Stalin said: "I'm going to send you to a collective farm...."[9]

---

[9] Variant: "Stalin, Roosevelt and Churchill were meeting, and in the middle of the road over which they were driving to their meeting place there was a bull which would not get off the road. First Roosevelt went up with his charming smile but the bull would not budge. Then Churchill went out and starting swearing at the ox and using his persuasive oratory, but en [sic] vain. Then Stalin went out and whispered something into the bull's ear. As soon as the bull heard it he took off and ran as far as he could. When Roosevelt and Churchill asked Stalin what he had told the bull he replied: 'I told him I would put him into a collective farm.'" HPSSS, no. 7, schedule A, vol. 1, 39; also no. 18, schedule A, vol. 2, 69; no. 24, schedule A, vol. 3, 51; no. 133, schedule A, vol. 10, 15.

The Early Postwar Years

Many in the USSR hoped that victory in 1945 would leave the Soviet government secure enough to abandon the heavy-handedness of the interwar period. Ordinary citizens felt they had proven themselves by resisting the Nazi onslaught and deserved credit for their service. Peasants hoped that the hated collective farms would be disbanded. Workers looked forward to a broader availability of consumer goods. Officers talked of having a greater say in national affairs. Members of the intelligentsia expressed an interest in a lifting of censorship at home and expanding contacts with colleagues abroad.[1] Needless to say, none of this ever came to pass—such expectations may have actually contributed to the party's reassertion of staunch ideological controls during the mid-to-late 1940s.

It is hard to know how Soviet society responded to this renewed repression. If the interwar period provides any clue, ordinary Soviets probably grumbled, kvetched, and dissembled as they had in times past. Such conclusions are difficult to document, however, due to the fragmentary nature of accessible information on Soviet political humor after 1945. This gap in the historical record is chiefly due to the postwar establishment of separate Allied occupation zones, which effectively halted the westward flight of Soviet refugees, deserting soldiers, and former *Ostarbeiter* slave laborers. Indeed, with the exception of a few defectors, all the former Soviets interviewed in the early 1950s by Evgenii Andreevich or the Harvard Project on the Soviet Social System had left the USSR before the end of the war. Perhaps this explains why the postwar jokes that they told diverge somewhat from contemporary concerns in Soviet society—by late 1945, Soviet refugees in central Europe had been cut off from their homeland and were no longer able to comment reliably on the postwar trajectory of Stalin-era political humor.

По глухой местности, сквозь лес, идёт молодая женщина с ребёнком на руках. За ней следом — офицер. Она прибавляет шагу — он тоже. Она почти бежит, он не отстаёт:	Deep in the woods, a young woman is walking with a baby in her arms. An officer follows her. She quickens her pace, but so does he. Soon she's almost running, but he manages to keep up with

---

[1] Elena Zubkova, *Russia After the War: Hopes, Illusions and Disappointments, 1945–1957*, trans. Hugh Ragsdale (Armonk, NY: M. E. Sharpe, 1998), 20–39.

—Ну, чего Вы так бежите, точно боитесь меня?

—Конечно, боюсь.

—Чего же Вы боитесь?

—Да Вы можете что угодно с беззащитной женщиной сделать. Изнасиловать можете....

—Помилуйте, во-первых, у меня нет такого намерения, во-вторых, у Вас ведь ребёнок на руках....

Женщина быстро:

—Так это ничего, ребёнка я могу на травку положить....

—Hey, why are you running? Are you afraid of me?

—Of course I'm scared.

—What are you scared of?

—Well, you could do whatever you please with a defenseless woman. You could rape her....

—My dear, I have no such intention and in any case, you have a baby in your arms....

The woman replies hastily:

—Well, that's nothing: I could always lay the baby down in the grass.[2]

★ ★ ★

В одной из вассальных стран, тотчас после её «освобождения» демонстрируется советский хроникальный фильм. На экране встреча Сталина с Бенешом. Сталин подходит к Бенешу с протянутой рукой, и в этот момент раздаётся возглас одного из кинозрителей:

—Давай часы.

Immediately after one of the new vassal states' "liberation," a Soviet newsreel was shown. Pictured on the screen was a meeting between Stalin and Beneš.[3] Just as Stalin is walking to Beneš with his hand extended, a voice from the audience calls out:

—Gimme your watch.[4]

★ ★ ★

На конференции четырёх министров иностранных дел великих держав— Англии, США, Франции и СССР в 1945 году министры беседуют и закуривают.

Бевин вынимает стильный дорогой портсигар, на котором выгравирована надпись: «Дорогому Бевину от

At a conference of the Big Four in 1945, the British, American, French, and Soviet foreign ministers started smoking during one of their discussions.

Bevin pulls out a stylish, expensive-looking cigarette case upon which is embossed: "To Our Dear Bevin, from

---

[2] The war left a profound gender imbalance in the USSR that was most visible in the countryside, where many villages were left without young men. Women wanting children are said to have agreed to the most temporary of liaisons in the hope of getting pregnant. A particularly grim variant notes that "there is a story current ... that all a girl has to do if she wants a man is to lie down on the main highway and stretch out her legs and hold up a liter of vodka in her arms." HPSSS, no. 133, schedule A, vol. 10, 26.

[3] Eduard Beneš (1884–1948), Czechoslovakian president, 1935–38, 1946–48.

[4] The reference is to Soviet troops' marauding and plunder during their postwar occupation of Eastern Europe.

благодарных профсоюзов».

Бернс вынимает портсигар с надписью: «Дорогому Бернсу от коллег-сенаторов».

Жорж Бидо открывает портсигар, маленький, изящный, золотой; видна гравировка: «Милому Жоржу от Сюзанны».

Наконец Молотов вытаскивает роскошный золотой портсигар, усеянный бриллиантами. Все взоры обращены на него. Раскрывает. Надпись: «Графу Потоцкому от князя Радзвила».

Your Grateful Trade Unions."

Byrnes produces a cigarette case with the engraving: "To Our Dear Byrnes, from Your Colleagues in the Senate."

Georges Bidault opens a cigarette case—a small, elegant one made of gold—which is embossed with: "To my sweet Georges, from Suzanna."[5]

Finally, Molotov produces a fine gold cigarette case, encrusted with diamonds. Everyone's eyes are drawn to it. As he opens it, they catch sight of the engraving, which reads: "To Count Potocki from Prince Radziwill."[6]

☆ ☆ ☆

В 1946, в связи с разгромом формализма и «торжеством» социалистического реализма, партийные фармацевты ходатайствовали о переименовании формалина в «соцреалин».

In 1946, formalism [in art, music, and literature] was routed in a major "victory" for Socialist Realism.[7] Party card-carrying pharmacists petitioned the state for permission to rename formaldehyde "socialist realdehyde."

☆ ☆ ☆

На заседании Политбюро обсуждается вопрос о немедленном завоевании «капиталистического мира». Берия предлагает:

—У нас есть 12 атомных бомб. Надо запаковать их в чемоданы, разослать по главным столицам и одновременно

One day, the Politburo is discussing the imminent defeat of the "capitalist world." Beriia[8] suggests:

—We have 12 atomic bombs. We should pack them into suitcases, sent them to the major capitals of the Western world, and set them to go off

---

[5] Ernest Bevin (1881–1951), labor leader and postwar British foreign secretary, 1945–51; James F. Byrnes (1879–1972), South Carolina senator and US secretary of state, 1945–47; Georges-Augustin Bidault (1899–1983), French foreign minister, 1944–46.

[6] Molotov's case was evidently a Polish heirloom looted during the 1944–45 Soviet occupation of Poland.

[7] The reference is to the 1946–47 campaign against modernism in music, which was launched alongside a larger drive for cultural orthodoxy known as the *Zhdanovshchina*.

[8] L. P. Beriia (1899–53), an infamous secret police chief and head of postwar nuclear program.

взорвать. Во время суматохи занимать нашей армией страну за страной.

Микоян протестует:

—План тов. Берия неосуществим. У нас не найдётся столько хороших чемоданов.

at the same instant. In the resulting confusion, our army could take one country after another.

Mikoian protests:

—Comrade Beriia's plan is not feasible. We don't have that many good suitcases.

Академик Лысенко демонстрировал аудитории результаты своих работ по изучению слуха у блохи. Он посадил блоху на правую руку и скомандовал:

—Прыгать на левую!

Блоха перепрыгнула на его левую руку. Он скомандовал снова:

—Прыгать на правую!

Блоха опять послушно перепрыгнула. Затем учёный осторожно оторвал задние ноги у блохи и скомандовал опять: «Прыгать на левую». Но блоха не пошевелилась. Он переложил блоху в другую руку и скомандовал «прыгать на правую», но и это не помогло.

—Можно считать диалектически научно доказанным,—сказал великий учёный,—что блоха вместе с ногами теряет слух.

Academician Lysenko[9] was demonstrating the results of his study of fleas' sense of hearing to a large audience. He sat a flea down in his right hand and commanded:

—Jump to the left!

The flea jumped onto his left hand. He commanded again:

—Jump to the right!

The flea again obediently made its jump. Then the scientist carefully tore off the flea's hind legs and repeated his command: "Jump to the left." The flea didn't move. He then took the flea and put it in his other hand and said "Jump to the right," but it didn't make any difference.

—We can thus consider it dialectically proven that when a flea loses its legs, it loses its sense of hearing as well.

Неустанно «заботясь о нуждах трудящихся», Сталин захотел однажды проверить, насколько народ стал покорным. Он объявил, что в такой-то день на Красной площади в Москве состоится «всенародное целование» его собственного зада. Пропаганда разъяснила, как именно народ должен ликовать и с каким энтузиазмом прикладываться.

Tirelessly "concerned with the well-being of the working class," Stalin decided one day to check just how subservient his people actually had become. He announced that on such-and-such a day, there would be a celebration on Red Square during which all of Moscow would be invited to kiss his ass. Propaganda accompanying the announcement dictated exactly how this

---

[9] T. D. Lysenko (1898–1976), a Soviet agronomist known for his fraudulent Marxist alternative to Mendel's system of hereditary genetics.

В назначенный день началась грандиозная демонстрация трудящихся, которые шли в стройных колоннах со знамёнами, транспорантами, плакатами и портретами «величайшего». Ярко блестел на солнце зад «родного, любимого», который стоял на лобном месте в нужной позе. «Организованно», в порядке очереди, люди подходили к «отцу народов» и, облобызав гениальный зад, отходили.

«Любимейший» оглядывался по сторонам: везде царили порядок, организованность, спокойствие — полная покорность.

И вдруг… в 20 шагах от «величайшего» началась какая-то заварушка — крики, ругань, скандал и свалка. Мигом вынырнули НКВДисты. Одна часть их стеною окружила «родного», а другая бросилась усмирять бунт.

Сам «гениальнейший» перевернулся, присел на корточки и начал дрожать от… храбрости. Но пара ударов, и порядок был восстановлен. От места свалки возвращается сияющий НКВДист.

was to take place and how people were to conduct themselves.

On the appointed day, a massive parade of workers marched in columns to Red Square with banners, flags, and portraits of the "great one." The "beloved one" assumed the necessary pose, his rear end shining brightly in the sun. Tightly organized into lines, people came up to the "father of the peoples," kissed his brilliant ass, and went on their way.

The "beloved one" looked from side to side: everywhere, there was order, discipline and calm—complete supplication.

Suddenly, only twenty paces away from the "great one," a disturbance erupted—yelling, shouts, swearing and fistfights. In an instant, the NKVD intervened. One contingent surrounded the "dear one," protecting him behind a human shield; the rest moved to suppress the unrest.

The "genius" turned over, crouched down, and shook from… bravery. Within a moment or two, however, order was restored. Beaming, an NKVD officer came up to Stalin from the scene of the

---

[10] A former Soviet citizen supplied a variant: "Stalin was amazed that the Russian people were so patient and uncomplaining. He decided that he would do them a favor and make them 'show their ego,' [that is] make them demonstrate their individuality in some way. So he ordered all butter to be taken away from the residents of Moscow. The day after the order was issued, the streets were absolutely quiet; not a single complaint was received. 'Tak! Tak! How far must we go to make the Russian people complain?' he wondered, and he next ordered all meat to be taken away. Still not a murmur. Astounded by their tolerance of hardship, he ordered all the bread taken away, too; the city was undisturbed. Finally he issued an order that everybody in the city was to be whipped ten times. The next morning, there was a great clamor in the streets, and Stalin sighed with relief and said, 'At last I have found something which will make the Russians complain, and I have given the people a chance to let their ego show!' But one of his aides said, 'No—look out the window. The people are fighting to get in line—and the scientific workers want to be taken out of turn!'" HPSSS, no. 610, schedule B, vol. 20, 2. For another variant, see Lyons, *Moscow Carousel*, 236–37.

—Ишьто слҷчылос?

—Все в порядке, Иосиф Виссарионович, просто Академия Наук хотела пролезть целовать без очереди.

incident. Stalin asked:

—So what happened?

—Everything is fine, Joseph Vissarionovich. It was just the Academy of Sciences, trying to jump the queue.[10]

В Москве после войны девушка по телефону услaвливается встретиться с молодым человеком, который её до того не видал. Тот спрашивает:

—А как Вас узнать? У Вас какие-нибудь отличительные признаки имеются?

—Как же: я буду без орденов и в новых галошах.

In Moscow after the war, a young woman agrees to go on a blind date with a fellow by telephone. He asks:

—How will I be able to recognize you? Is there anything unusual about the way you look?

—Of course. I'll be in new galoshes and won't be wearing any of my medals.[11]

[11] Such modesty in regard to decorations was rare. For a prewar variant, see HPSSS, no. 127, schedule A, vol. 10, 16.

Appendix

Jokes from the Harvard Project on the Soviet Social System

Between 1950 and 1951, the Harvard Project on the Soviet Social System interviewed over 300 former Soviet citizens in an effort to assess the nature and extent of social support for the Stalinist regime. Participants were recruited from among ethnic Russians, Ukrainians, Belorussians, and other former Soviets in West Germany—mostly former POWs, *Ostarbeiter* laborers, and Nazi collaborators who had managed to avoid repatriation to the USSR at the end of the war. The Harvard Project aspired to use a battery of sociological interview questionnaires to map these former Soviets' views on authority and ideology, as well as their experiences in the workplace, at home and in society at large.

Historically, the results of the Harvard Project have been difficult to use and interpret because even though the researchers collected basic information about their informants, they also guaranteed them anonymity in order to ease concerns that participation in the study might endanger family and friends still in the USSR. These concerns precluded the recording or professional transcription of the interviews; instead, researchers took detailed notes in shorthand (often in Russian or Ukrainian) and then summarized and translated these scribblings into a primitive dictaphone for later transcription. Although this unusual way of establishing rapport with the project's participants yielded fascinating information about Soviet society, it did so at the cost of failing to preserve a precise record of the way in which the survey informants expressed their revelations.[1]

Today, the project's "transcripts" remain as they did in the early 1950s and consist of uncorrected, often clumsy translations, littered with mistakes and misunderstandings. That said, they form an incredibly rich repository of raw information on aspects of Stalin-era social history, including political humor. Many interviewers asked their informants about joke-telling under Stalin and recorded what they learned with relish. An ideal source for verifying the authenticity of the jokes published in Andreevich's collection, the Harvard Project also contains several dozen unique jokes that do not appear in *The Kremlin and the People*. They are reproduced on the pages that follow and cross-referenced against other sources whenever possible.

---

[1] Regrettably, the interviewers' shorthand notes were not preserved.

Party Leaders

Stalin went to Georgia on a vacation. There, on a road, he saw a peasant driving a donkey. The donkey stopped and didn't want to go on. The man pushed and screamed and yelled, but the donkey wouldn't move. Stalin said: "You are a very bad leader. You only have one donkey and you can't even get it to move. I have 200 million donkeys and they all listen to me."[2]

Churchill came to Moscow to see Stalin. They argued. Each said that his people live better than the other. Suddenly out of a window, they saw a Jew dancing. Stalin pointed out the Jew to Churchill: "See how happy the Soviet people are." Then he brought the Jew to the Kremlin and Churchill asked him "Why are you so happy? Why are you dancing?" The Jew said "Why not? I received a pound of sugar and I can still get another pound."[3]

[During] the holiday in October, the Cheka was thinking of ideas how to make people happy. Someone proposed to give the people a pound of sugar. Another said "Give them something else," the third one said "Give them still something else" but none of these suggestions was considered good. Finally a Jew got up and said "Give me 5 rubles and I will make the people happy." They all sat back in amazement and wondered how he could do this. So the Jew said "well I would take the 5 rubles and with it send a telegram to all the people saying Stalin is dead. And this would make the people happy."[4]

A foreigner came to talk with Stalin and asked him: "...They say that Voroshilov and Shvernik[5] are not very capable... why do you put them in high positions?" Stalin said nothing, but got up, took one telephone and put it on the floor. Then he took another telephone and put it on the windowsill. The visitor asked: "Why did you do this?" and the answer was "my telephones I can put where I please. My fools I can also put where I please."[6]

[2] HPSSS, no. 25, schedule A, vol. 3, 68.

[3] HPSSS, no. 1, schedule A, vol. 1, 25.

[4] HPSSS, no. 1, schedule A, vol. 1, 25.

[5] N. M. Shvernik (1888–1970), a party hierarch.

[6] HPSSS, no. 64, schedule A, vol. 6, 67. For a variant, see Lyons, *Moscow Carousel*, 334–35.

Three heads of state once got together.... Let's say France, Russia, and Germany. They began to argue. Whose soldiers will fulfill an order, no matter what [...]? To settle the argument they brought in three soldiers and opened up a window on, let's say, the fifth floor. Then they said to the French soldier; "Jump out of the window." The French soldier looked around and said: "What for? I have a wife and children. I don't want to jump out." So they [...] told the German: "Jump out of the window. He too asked "Why?" and refused to do it. [...] Then they told a Russian soldier: "Jump out of the window." Without saying a word he got up and started to jump. They grabbed him by the seat of his pants, pulled him back and asked him: "Why is it that you will obey that order without even thinking about it?" And he answered: "Well, to me it wouldn't make any difference. I have already lost my life."[7]

[At] an inventors' congress, everybody tells about his greatest accomplishments. The Americans bring up the hydrogen bombs, the British and the Spanish something else. Then the Russian says: "But we have the greatest inventors of all. Comrade Stalin [...] has done the impossible in transmutation of matter. He takes some dirt, blows on it, and it becomes a marshal. And he takes a marshal, and blows on him, and he becomes dirt.[8]

Stalin died, and the Politburo began to discuss [...] which Tsar they should bury Stalin next to. They decided to put him next to Peter the Great. Peter rose from his grave and said: "Go away, I opened a window to Europe and you closed it." Then they carried Stalin's body to the grave of Alexander II. He also refused to accept him, telling him: "I liberated the peasants and you enslaved them. Go away." Then they went to Nicholas II, and he said: "I cannot lie next to you, I gave the people vodka and something to eat with it, and then you did not even give them something to eat." Then they took him to Catherine [the Great]. "Alright," she said, let's go sleep together; in my years I have slept with many a good for nothing."[9]

[7] HPSSS, no. 18, schedule A, vol. 2, 74–75; also no. 628, schedule A, vol. 29, 30–31.

[8] A reference to G. K. Zhukov and other Red Army commanders demoted after the end of the Second World War. HPSSS, no. 133, schedule A, vol. 10, 30. For earlier variants, see the diary entry from March 7, 1928 in Shitts, *Dnevnik "Velikogo pereloma,"* 2; HPSSS, no. 522, schedule A, vol. 27, 33; p. 59, n. 17.

[9] HPSSS, no. 64, schedule A, vol. 66, 67.

FIGURE 34. Kalinin on an official visit to the Kuban region

Kalinin decided once to find out how the peasants lived. He went to the country, left his [car] somewhere, and walked on a road. He overtook a kolkhoznik, who was riding on a cart with a horse. Kalinin asked him to give him a ride and the kolkhoznik said "Of course." The cart had wooden axels, very badly greased, as grease was not available. The kolkhoznik talked about this lack of grease and he stopped the horse, went to the side of the road, took his pants off, and relieved himself. Then he took a spade and began to spread what he had produced on the axels. Kalinin asked him, "What are you doing?" The answer was: "Can't you see? I have to grease the axels." Kalinin said "But this is not grease." And the kolkhoznik answered: *"Kakaia vlast', takaia i maz'* [Edverything else is shit, so why should this be different?]."[10]

MTS—Machine Tractor Station
Mausoleum To Stalin (*Mogila tovarishchu Stalinu*).[11]

✯ ✯ ✯

[T]he Soviet leaders were attending a party given by President Roosevelt in his temporary headquarters in the Crimea during the Yalta Conference.

---

[10] HPSSS, no. 66, schedule A, vol. 6, 67; also no. 46, schedule A, vol. 4, 49.

[11] HPSSS, no. 24, schedule A, vol. 3, 51; no. 479, schedule A, vol. 24, 23; no. 481, schedule A, vol. 24, 38; no. 524, schedule A, vol. 27, 44.

Stalin noticed that during the dinner, Kalinin carefully examined two silver spoons which were laying on the table next to his place and carefully placed them in his vest pocket. Stalin tapped on his glass and explained that he was about to perform a very clever trick: he took two teaspoons from his place and put them in his vest pocket and then declared: "Now, behold, the teaspoons are not longer in my pocket, but in the pocket of Kalinin." All eyes turned toward Kalinin and Kalinin, like a trained dog, laid the spoons back on the table.[12]

Kalinin was visited by the Turkish president Kemal Pasha[13] and his wife. Kalinin took the Pasha's wife to the Moscow opera and she sat next to him and he very flatteringly talked to her. Suddenly he thought he saw a thread hanging down on the hem of her skirt. So, he very obligingly wanted to pull it off and he started pulling and pulling and it continued. Well, once he started he could not stop and so he continued rolling up the thread which continued [to stretch] longer and longer. The next day Kemal Pasha came to thank Kalinin for his hospitality. He said [his wife thought] the performance was wonderful but [also] says: "I really didn't think things went this far in your country. I knew there were thieves but I never imagined it possible that somebody would have taken the panties off my wife at an opera performance."[14]

Kalinin, when he got married, got married to a young singer, and before he got married he went to a doctor in order to get himself examined and see what his state of general health was. The doctor wrote a little piece of paper, saying that he was MTS. Of course, Kalinin was very satisfied with this, but when he got married he just couldn't do anything to his wife. You know, he was a little bit old. Then he went back to the doctor and asked him, why it is so, I mean, you wrote down MTS. It means Machine Tractor Station and I thought I was such a strong man like a tractor. The doctor answered, no, no, I just wrote: "*Mozhet tol'ko sosat'*" [Maximum: Touch and Suck].[15]

---

[12] HPSSS, no. 534, schedule A, vol. 28, 23–24.

[13] Mustafa Kemal Pasha Ataturk (1881–1938), an early Turkish nationalist and founder of modern Turkey.

[14] HPSSS, no. 56, schedule A, vol. 5, 46–47.

[15] A jokester apparently got five years in prison for this joke. HPSSS, no. 285, schedule A, vol. 15, 15.

Molotov went to Kalinin with the complaint that his testicles were so weak that he could no longer have sexual relations. Kalinin told him that he had once had the same trouble but had gone to a certain doctor in Paris who had given him a new pair of testicles and that he was now fine. So, Kalinin gave Molotov the address of this doctor in Paris and Molotov went there. The doctor amputated Molotov's testicles and told him, that he would give him a new pair, taken from a chimpanzee. Molotov returned to Moscow but a little while later went back to see Kalinin. He told him that he was no better off than before. Kalinin asked Molotov to take down his pants and he carefully inspected Molotov's new testicles. The he looked up and told him: "Do you know what that doctor did? He gave you my old testicles."[16]

[At] a meeting in which Kalinin and Stalin were present, Kalinin was scratching himself very vigorously throughout the meeting. Stalin asked him what was the matter and Kalinin said that he had fleas. Thereupon Stalin advised him to put up a sign: "Kolkhozes being organized," and all the fleas disappeared.[17]

---

[16] Uncomfortable with the ribald nature of this joke, the respondent who recounted it asked that it not be included in the interviewer's final Harvard Project report. HPSSS, no. 110, schedule A, vol. 8, 24.

[17] HPSSS, no. 118, schedule A, vol. 9, 17. Variant: "Stalin had a case of the crabs (*mandovoshki*) and he called Molotov to him and said to Molotov: 'Hey, Molotov, look here, look at this terrible business (*bezobrazie*). What can be done?' Molotov took out his microscope and looked carefully, and then straightened up and said to Stalin 'Take a piece of chalk and draw a line around it, and mark it kolkhoz. And then all the crabs will run away.'" HPSSS, no. 60, schedule A, vol. 5, 33; no. 62, schedule A, vol. 5, 26. Another variant: "I now remember a Soviet anecdote... about the unsanitary conditions in the prison I was in from 1937 to 1939. If someone found on himself a group of bedbugs, we would say, show them a kolkhoz and they will quickly disperse." HPSSS, no. 102, schedule A, vol. 8, 64. Still another: "The all-popular inhabitants of the Kremlin were attacked by body-lice, as persistent as one of the Egyptian plagues. Scientists were helpless. Finally Karl Radek—to whom all such witticisms are automatically and quite unfairly attributed—made a suggestion that saved the day: 'Collectivize them,' he is supposed to have said, 'then half of them will die and the other half will run away.'" Lyons, *Moscow Carousel*, 334. For another variant, see Talmadge, "The Enjoyment of Laughter in Russia," 50–51.

FIGURE 35. Statue to Minin and Pozharskii, Red Square

Minin says to Pozharsky after the erection of Lenin's tomb:

Smotri-ka, kniaz', kakaia griaz',	Oh Prince, such gall! The shame of it all!
U sten kremlevskikh uleglas'.	The filth they've piled by the Kremlin wall.[18]

---

[18] The reference is to I. Martos's 1818 Red Square statue to Kuz'ma Minin (d. 1616) and Prince Dmitrii Pozharskii (1578–1642), who are traditionally credited with liberating Moscow from the Poles in 1612–13. See HPSSS, no. 11, schedule A, vol. 2, 50. A more elaborate version of this couplet was uncovered in the Leningrad mail:

Minin: I skazhi mne kniaz',	Minin: Prince, Prince, explain it all!
Chto tam za mraz',	Such shame! Such gall!
U sten Kremlevskikh zavelas'.	Such a pile of filth they've piled by the Kremlin wall.
Pozharskii: Na meste kazni Pugacheva	Pozharskii: Where Pugachev got what he deserves,
Lezhit konservy iz Il'icha,	They've made Lenin into preserves,
Ved' on pri zhizni byl messiia.	After all, in life he was a saint,
I blagodarnaia Rossiia,	And whatever Russians are, ungrateful they ain't,
Pod gimnov i mortir,	So with mortar and a sorrowful scene,
Spustila Lenina v s[ortir].	They've buried him in a latrine.

A kolkhoznik comes to Moscow and is walking around on the street [when] he has to go to the bathroom. There were not enough public bathrooms in Moscow and sometimes you could see 20 or 30 people standing in line [...]. Now not far from the Lubianka there stands a statue of the first man to print a book in Russia, Ivan Fedorov.[19] In his hand he is holding a sheet of paper [...T]he kolkhoznik comes up the statue and said "Ivan Fedorov, this is the first time I have been in Moscow. Could you tell me where I could find a bathroom?" The statue looked down at him and said, "I've had the paper for all these years, but I myself still do not know where to go."

So the kolkhoznik walks on a little further. Next to the Bolshoi Theater there stands a little art theater[20] and opposite is a statue of Ostrovskii, [...] sitting in a big armchair.[21] The kolkhoznik goes up and asks him if he knows where he can find a bathroom. Ostrovskii answers him, "I am thankful that I have my chair here, because I would not know where to go myself."

The kolkhoznik walks on a little further and comes to Pushkin Square where there stands a statue of Pushkin. Pushkin has one hand in his jacket and is holding a stove pipe hat behind him with his other hand. The kolkhoznik asks him, if he knows where there is a bathroom. Pushkin answers, "I have never bothered to look for one. I have my hat handy right here."

So the kolkhoznik walks on and comes to the Red Square [...] monument to Minin and Pozharsky. Pozharsky is shown sitting down while Minin is standing next to him with one hand around Pozharsky's shoulders and the other [...] pointing toward the Mausoleum and Lenin. The kolkhoznik says, "Comrade, I cannot go any further. You must tell me where I can find a bathroom." Minin looks down at him, then gestures with his outstretched hand and says *"Pozhaluista" [Voila]."*[22]

Everyday Life

[In the 1920s, the regime attempted to undermine the "bourgeois" institution of marriage. During those years, there was a man and wife.] This is the way they live: She is in Moscow and he is Siberia, and they make love to

---

See TsGAIPD SPb f. 16, op. 5, d. 5912, l. 131 (the editor is grateful to Olga Velikanova for supplying this information). For other variants, see "Sovetskie anekdoty," 55; HPSSS, no. 5, schedule A, vol. 1, 18.

[19] A sixteenth-century artisan credited with introducing the printing press into Muscovy.

[20] Reference to the Malyi Theater.

[21] A. N. Ostrovskii (1823–86), a playwright.

[22] HPSSS, no. 385, schedule A, vol. 19, 25–26.

each other by telegraph. But there are children. Whom do the children resemble? They resemble the clerk at the corner drug-store."[23]

☆ ☆ ☆

A woman went to a doctor and asked him to give her some advice, saying that every time a man touched her she became pregnant. He said that he will give her some paste [sic, cream]. She replied that once she used such a paste and she had one child.

—Alright, he said, I will prescribe a douche.

—Well, she said, I used that too and then I had two children.

—Well, maybe you should try the diaphragm.

—Oh doctor, when I used that I had three children.

The doctor was a bit taken aback and told her to let her man wear a contraceptive. To this she replied that he wears two and that they usually break with a huge noise. In desperation the doctor said:

—Well, why don't you drink some Narzan. Narzan is a mineral water that comes from the Caucasus.

—Oh yes, how wonderful, when shall I drink it, before or after?

—During [sic, Instead of].[24]

☆ ☆ ☆

What is the difference between a *konfetka* [a piece of candy] and a *piatiletka* [a Five-Year Plan]? A person sucks a piece of candy till it is dry while a five-year plan sucks a person till he is dry.[25]

☆ ☆ ☆

Engineers were in the worst position of all during [the purges]. There was an anecdote current then: two old men met and one asked the other, "Well, how are things with you?" The other replied, "Bad, my son has just been arrested." And the first man said, "Gosh—my son is an engineer too."[26]

☆ ☆ ☆

Stakhanovites do not work with enthusiasm but just for the advantage they receive. There's an anecdote. A big line of people is waiting to receive goods at a store. An old half deaf lady comes up and asks, "What are they giving?" (*Chto daiut?*) You see we never say, "They sell"; they "give." So a man in line says "In the mug" (*po morde*). The old lady answers, no hearing

---

[23] HPSSS, no. 105, schedule A, vol. 8, 31.

[24] Evidently, the HPSSS interviewer misunderstood the punch line "Instead of" (*vmesto*) as "During" (*vmeste*). See HPSSS, no. 1158, schedule B, vol. 22, 34–35.

[25] HPSSS, no. 1495, schedule A, vol. 35, 35.

[26] HPSSS, no. 403, schedule B, vol. 20, 18.

FIGURE 36. Stalin. Factory mechanic at home

well, "To everyone, or just to the Stakhanovites?" You see, Stakhanovites always get first choice and the rest of the people get only what is left.[27]

[State] loan subscriptions [were widely publicized and it was obligatory to subscribe...] A little boy of six asks his father for a ruble. His father answered "Why?" He said: "For women." "What do you mean, for women, you are only six years old." The boy said "For Spanish women."[28]

There was a joke about [collective farmers' chronically low wages]: one kolkhoznik asked another: "how do you manage to earn so much money?" The other kolkhoznik answers: "I work twenty five hours each day." The first

---

[27] HPSSS, no. 1486, schedule A, vol. 34, 19.

[28] A reference to the collection of humanitarian aid to be sent to republican forces and refugees during the Spanish Civil War. HPSSS no. 5, schedule A, vol. 1, 24. Variant: "Contributing to various campaigns started at an early age, all children were used to it. A joke which was popular: a little boy begging his father to give him a ruble: 'Daddy, I need money for Spanish women [na ispanskikh zhenshchin].'" HPSSS, no. 3, schedule A, vol. 1, 32.

kolkhoznik said: "How can this be, there are only twenty four hours in a day." And the second kolkhoznik replied: "But I get up an hour earlier."[29]

There is a reason why the NKVD has a uniform that is blue with green striping. That is because after you get beaten up you are blue all over with green streaks....[30]

Both the tsarist and the Soviet currency is marked "State Credit Certificate" [*Gosudarstvennyi kreditnyi bilet*]. The joke is to fold a bill in such a way that [...] only the following is showing: "*Go-vennyi kreditnyi bilet*" [S[h]it Certificate].[31]

A man stands in front of a wall-[news]paper and reads the paper and says: "Oh, how they press [sic, squeeze]!" (*zhmut*). Behind him, a Party man walks up to him and asks him: "Who [is squeezing you]?" The man answers: "Uh, my shoes..." "But you don't have any..." [T]he man replies: "Well, that's why I don't wear any...."[32]

[After the war,] a colonel and a priest were riding together on the train. They were... admiring [each other's regalia—especially] the priest's cross and the officer's epaulettes. Finally the officer asked the priest: "Where did you get your cross? to which the priest replied: "Where did you get your epaulettes?" The officer retorted: "The government gave them to me." So the priest: "The government gave me the cross too."[33]

Jewish and Ethnic Stereotyping

When you have one German, or where there is one German, he is a philosopher; two Germans, you have an organization; three Germans, a war. When you have one Frenchman, he is a hero; two Frenchmen, you have love, three Frenchmen, you have marriage, that is the marriage of the husband, the

---

[29] HPSSS, no. 110, schedule A, vol. 8, 50.

[30] HPSSS, no. 133, schedule A, vol. 10, 23.

[31] A jokester was exiled for this joke, variants of which date to before 1917. HPSSS, no. 1053, schedule A, vol. 31, 16.

[32] HPSSS, no. 133, schedule A, vol. 10, 48.

[33] HPSSS, no. 133, schedule A, vol. 10, 35. For similar grumbling among workers in 1943 about the revival of old regime regalia—"first epaulettes, then priests and now the [closure of the] Comintern"—see RGASPI f. 17, op. 125, d. 181, ll. 2, 4.

wife and the friend of the wife. When you have one Italian you have a tenor; two Italians, burglars; three Italians, a retreat. When you have one Englishman, you have a sportsman, two Englishmen, a club; three Englishmen, Great Britain. When you have one Russian, you have a melancholic; two Russians, a marriage, but you know typically, people don't get along very well with each other in a Russian marriage; and when you have three Russians, you have a revolution.[34]

A lady was traveling on a British ship. This lady stood one day on the deck. A sailor stood on the desk below, looking up at her. At that moment, a gust of wind lifted her skirt high up. The lady noticed that the sailor had not stopped looking at her and in a rage went to the captain to protest against the impossible behavior of the sailor. The captain told her that he would look into the matter. The next morning the whole ship and this lady were shocked to read on the bulletin board that a particular sailor had been sentenced to 25 years at hard labor. Our lady, deeply pained at this grossly excessive punishment rushed again to the captain and asked him to explain why he had punished the sailor so severely. The captain answered that he had spent the night going over the maritime code, looking for an article which would fit the case. While he was unable to find an article specifically meeting the requirements, he discovered one which said in effect that a sailor, finding himself on the high seas and seeing an open hole without plugging it, would be punished with 25 years of hard labor![35]

During the [civil] war between the Reds and Makhno[36] and other bandits, they once captured a little Armenian, and they asked him which side he prefers. He pointed to the road where a large pile of manure had been divided in two by the wheel of a wagon. He said, which of those piles to you prefer?[37]

    ★ ★ ★

A man was riding in a train filled with other people, including one militia man. Suddenly, this man began to make indecent noises. The militia man fined him 5 rubles at which point an Armenian, sitting in the compartment, asked the militia man "Why?" The militia man replied: "For disturbing the public peace and quiet." "Yes," the Armenian asked, "but where does that money go?" Answered the militia man: "For construction to fulfill our

[34] HPSSS, no. 14, schedule A, vol. 2, 52.

[35] HPSSS, no. 1069, schedule A, vol. 31, 70–71.

[36] Nestor Makhno (1888–1934), a Ukrainian anarchist leader during the civil war.

[37] HPSSS, no. 102, schedule A, vol. 8, 65.

program." Then the Armenian replied: "But how much hot air does it take to build socialism?"[38]

A Jew called up the NKVD office and asked, "Please, what time is it?" "It is two o'clock," he was told. Fifteen minutes later he called again and said, "What time is it?" "It is 2:15", he was told. A little while later he called up again and asked "What time is it?" The NKVD man became quite annoyed and said "Why are you calling here to find out the time? Why don't you call the office of the city Soviet or the post office? Why here?" And the Jew replied "well where else can I call, since you have my gold watch."[39]

Three Jews volunteered for the Finnish Front. On the way north they were singing the "Song of the Three Tank Drivers." When they reached Leningrad, they changed the song and began to sing "The Clouds are over the City and the Air is Full of Electricity." When they reached the Finnish front, they changed their song again: "Be Healthy and Live Well—We are Leaving for Home."[40]

There is an old proverb about a director who wanted [to hire] a cashier. So he called a Russian and asked him "Do you know anything about being a cashier?" The Russian answered: "Yes, why not?" The director asked him: "How much is 2 and 2?" The Russian answered "4." The director said that is no good. Then the director called a Jew and asked him "How much are 2 and 2?" And the Jew answered: "How much do you want?" And so the director hired the Jew.[41]

A Jewish tailor received a visit from a finance inspector. Such visits took place every four months. He asked the tailor how things were and how much he had earned in the last quarter. The tailor answered that things were bad indeed since there was little cloth, and that he had earned only the following

---

[38] HPSSS, no. 7 schedule A, vol. 1, 39.

[39] HPSSS, no. 9, schedule A, vol. 1, 116.

[40] HPSSS, no. 1493, schedule A, vol. 35, 17. The references are to "Tri tankista," from the film *The Tractor Drivers* (*Traktoristy*, I. Pyr'ev, 1937) by B. Laskin and the Pokrass brothers; "Tuchi nad gorodom vstali," from the film *Man with a Gun* (*Chelovek s ruzhem*, S. I. Iutkevich, 1938) by P. Armand; "Byvaite zdorovy, zhivite bogato," from *Concert on the Silver Screen* (*Kontsert na ekrane*, A. N. Andrievskii, 1940) by A. G. Rusak, M. Isakovskii, and V. Zakharov.

[41] HPSSS, no. 60, schedule A, vol. 5, 25. See also no. 26, schedule B, vol. 3, 16; no. 403, schedule B, vol. 4, 11.

sum. He was then told by the inspector that he would have to pay half the sum he earned as a tax. The tailor told him that it would be impossible for him to pay such a sum, but, as he was threatened with closure, he agreed. The next time the inspector came, the tailor told him he had earned half of the sum he had indicated the last time. He was then told to pay three times that sum, and if he did not, he would go to jail. The tailor was not particularly worried as he had started to print his own money. The next time he was told by the inspector to pay 20,000 rubles in taxes since he had been able to pay the tax the last time. The tailor printed money furiously and delivered the sum in due time. When the next quarter had passed, he was informed that his tax would now be 50,000 rubles. The tailor was desperate as he no longer had enough paper to print the whole sum. As a result, he was unable to pay. The next day when the inspector came to arrest him as he had defaulted, the tailor showed him the machine and what paper he had left and told him to take it all.[42]

---

[42] HPSSS, no. 1069, schedule A, vol. 31, 74–75.